Life Changing Quotes

for

Gratitude,
Health,
Happiness,
and
Wealth.

David Sparks

Contents

Introduction

Quotes seem to have a magical quality about them. For some reason, many people love reading them. Maybe its because the words speak to the person or maybe because they like and admire the author. Either way, quotes seem to carry an energy of their own, like a call to action.

Quotes can be inspirational to many, however just as many are not inspired. This may have to do with timing. When a reader reads a quote, they may not be in the appropriate state of mind, or the appropriate stage in their life to appreciate the meaning or lessons behind the words.

As a teacher I have displayed quite a few quotes around my classroom with the hope that one of them will inspire the students and motivate them to work that little bit harder. I was truly amazed when I received a phone call from parents of a student, thanking me for what I had said in class one day. These parents had been having difficulty with their 15-year-old son for quite some time, but he did a turn around after reading one of the new quotes I had put up in the room. The quote was **"time is all you've got and time is running out."** I had heard it while listening to a Jim Rohn tape and thought it would be useful to the students, as school would finish before they knew it.

The quotes written in this book are specifically about Gratitude, Health, Happiness, and Wealth, as I believe these are four of the most important areas of life, (and in this order). Gratitude comes first, because you have to be thankful for what you've got. I think Oprah says it best and hers is the first quote of this compilation.

The words in this book come from actors and actresses, athletes, businessmen and women, politicians, musicians, philosophers, scientists and more. Some quotes go back as far as ancient Rome and ancient Greece and are still relevant to this day.

I suggest this book be used as a regular 'go to', so keep it handy and look at it often. You may read something now which may not resonate with you at this point in your life, but a year or two down the track, it will have a totally different meaning.

You will notice that a few quotes sound the same, but come from different authors. I have put this down to the individuals being on the same wavelength and their experiences having led them to formulate similar beliefs.

Of course, you probably won't find every quote useful or inspiring, but this is to be expected. Since everyone's values are different, different quotations will inspire different people.

Hopefully you will enjoy these quotes for a long time to come and notice the improvements that benefit your life by making the small changes that these sages provoke.

Gratitude

Be thankful for what you have; you'll end up having more. If you concentrate on what you don't have, you will never, ever have enough.

- Oprah Winfrey

Do not regret growing older, it is a privilege denied to many.

- Unknown

Make it a habit to tell people thank you. To express your appreciation, sincerely and without the expectation of anything in return. Truly appreciate those around you, and you'll soon find many others around you. Truly appreciate life, and you'll find that you have more of it.

- Ralph Marston

'Thank you' is the best prayer that anyone could say. I say that one a lot. Thank you expresses extreme gratitude, humility, understanding.

- Alice Walker

Appreciation is the highest form of prayer, for it acknowledges the presence of good wherever you shine the light of your thankful thoughts.

- Alan Cohen

Be grateful for what you have and stop complaining - it bores everybody else, does you no good, and doesn't solve any problems.

- Zig Ziglar

Gratitude is the sign of noble souls.

- Aesop

Thank you for life, and all the little ups and downs that make it worth living.

- Travis Barker

I don't need a holiday or a feast to feel grateful for my children, the sun, the moon, the roof over my head, music, and laughter, but I like to take this time to take the path of thanks less travelled.

- Paula Poundstone

When a person doesn't have gratitude, something is missing in his or her humanity.

- Elie Wiesel

None of us got to where we are alone. Whether the assistance we received was obvious or subtle, acknowledging someone's help is a big part of understanding the importance of saying thank you.

- Harvey Mackay

Gratitude makes sense of our past, brings peace for today, and creates a vision for tomorrow.

- Melody Beattie

Gratitude unlocks the fullness of life. It turns what we have into enough, and more. It turns denial into acceptance, chaos to order, confusion to clarity. It can turn a meal into a feast, a house into a home, a stranger into a friend.

- Melody Beattie

All I ever wanted really, and continue to want out of life, is to give 100 percent to whatever I'm doing and to be committed to whatever I'm doing and then let the results speak for themselves. Also to never take myself or people for granted and always be thankful and grateful to the people who helped me.

- Jackie Joyner-Kersee

When you rise in the morning, give thanks for the light, for your life, for your strength. Give thanks for your food and for the joy of living. If you see no reason to give thanks, the fault lies in yourself.

- **Tecumseh**

No one who achieves success does so without acknowledging the help of others. The wise and confident acknowledge this help with gratitude.

- **Alfred North Whitehead**

Gratitude bestows reverence, allowing us to encounter everyday epiphanies, those transcendent moments of awe that change forever how we experience life and the world.

- **John Milton**

Some people are always grumbling because roses have thorns; I am thankful that thorns have roses.

- **Alphonse Karr**

When you practice gratefulness, there is a sense of respect toward others.

- **Dalai Lama**

If the only prayer you ever say in your entire life is thank you, it will be enough.

— **Meister Eckhart**

When it comes to life the critical thing is whether you take things for granted or take them with gratitude.

— **Gilbert K. Chesterton**

Keep your eyes open to your mercies. The man who forgets to be thankful has fallen asleep in life.

— **Robert Louis Stevenson**

Thankfulness is the beginning of gratitude. Gratitude is the completion of thankfulness. Thankfulness may consist merely of words. Gratitude is shown in acts.

— **Henri Frederic Amiel**

When I started counting my blessings, my whole life turned around.

— **Willie Nelson**

When you are grateful - when you can see what you have - you unlock blessings to flow in your life.

— **Suze Orman**

I would maintain that thanks are the highest form of thought, and that gratitude is happiness doubled by wonder.

- Gilbert K. Chesterton

God has two dwellings; one in heaven, and the other in a meek and thankful heart.

- Izaak Walton

I've been giving back since I was a teen, handing out turkeys at Thanksgiving and handing out toys at toys drives for Christmas. It's very important to give back as a youth. It's as simple as helping an old lady across the street or giving up your seat on the bus for someone who is pregnant.

- Queen Latifah

I give all the glory to God. It's kind of a win-win situation. The glory goes up to Him and the blessings fall down on me.

- Gabby Douglas

Gratitude is not only the greatest of virtues, but the parent of all the others.

- Marcus Tullius Cicero

There's no happier person than a truly thankful, content person.

- Joyce Meyer

Of all the characteristics needed for both a happy and morally decent life, none surpasses gratitude. Grateful people are happier, and grateful people are more morally decent.

- Dennis Prager

If you suffer, thank God! It is a sure sign that you are alive.

- Elbert Hubbard

I'm very thankful to be doing what I'm doing. I feel very blessed.

- Justin Timberlake

I'm thankful to be breathing, on this side of the grass. Whatever comes, comes.

- Ron Perlman

Gratitude is the most exquisite form of courtesy.

- Jacques Maritain

I am what I am, I'm doing very well in my life, and I'm thankful to God for that.

- L. L Cool J

I work very hard, and I play very hard. I'm grateful for life. And I live it - I believe life loves the liver of it. I live it.

- Maya Angelou

Gratitude changes the pangs of memory into a tranquil joy.

- Dietrich Bonhoeffer

Be thankful for problems. If they were less difficult, someone with less ability might have your job.

- Jim Lovell

The hardest arithmetic to master is that which enables us to count our blessings.

- Eric Hoffer

Gratitude is the fairest blossom which springs from the soul.

- Henry Ward Beecher

Does not the gratitude of the dog put to shame any man who is ungrateful to his benefactors?

- Saint Basil

I wouldn't change anything. I've made mistakes, but thanks to those mistakes, I've learned.

- Enrique Iglesias

I'm thankful for weird people out there 'cause they're some of the most creative people.

- Channing Tatum

It's been quite a roller coaster ride, but I've grown and learned a lot about myself. The greatest thing is being able to interact with fans and touch people's lives... for that I give thanks.

- Christina Aguilera

Gratitude is a duty which ought to be paid, but which none have a right to expect.

- Jean-Jacques Rousseau

Well, there's not a day goes by when I don't get up and say thank you to somebody.

- Rod Stewart

Charity never humiliated him who profited from it, nor ever bound him by the chains of gratitude, since it was not to him but to God that the gift was made.

- Antoine de Saint-Exupery

I'm thankful for the incredible advances in medicine that have taken place during my lifetime. I almost certainly wouldn't still be here if it weren't for them.

- Billy Graham

I'm thankful for serendipitous moments in my life, where things could've gone the other way.

- Rick Springfield

When you solve a problem, you ought to thank God and go on to the next one.

- Dean Rusk

Dear Lord, I'm so grateful I'm still loved.

- Vivien Leigh

No duty is more urgent than that of returning thanks.

- James Allen

Sometimes we need to remind ourselves that thankfulness is indeed a virtue.

- William Bennett

Whatever life throws at me I'll take it and be grateful for it as well.

- Tom Felton

A single grateful thought toward heaven is the most perfect prayer.

- Gotthold Ephraim Lessing

The brave who focus on all things good and all things beautiful and all things true, even in the small, who give thanks for it and discover joy even in the here and now, they are the change agents who bring fullest Light to all the world.

- Ann Voskamp

A proud man is seldom a grateful man, for he never thinks he gets as much as he deserves.

- Henry Ward Beecher

I am thankful that geniuses and artists and good people, no matter how hard it is, will eventually be recognized. I am doubly thankful that also goes for idiots.

- Elayne Boosler

Immensely grateful, touched, proud, astonished, abashed.

- Boris Pasternak

We sing a little song before we eat, a little blessing before we eat, and it's really - we're thanking the Lord and the Earth for the food that we eat, and it really brings you together in a profound kind of way.

- Phil Lesh

I'm grateful for my brokenness. I'm grateful for my humility.

- James McGreevey

I have nothing to ask for, thanks to God. Everything I have, God has given me.

- Mariano Rivera

I am thankful, of course, for the prize and thankful to God for each story, each idea, each word, each day.

- Isaac Bashevis Singer

Old age is not a matter for sorrow. It is matter for thanks if we have left our work done behind us.

– **Thomas Carlyle**

Like Christ said, love thee one another. I learned to do that, and I learned to respect and be appreciative and thankful for what I had.

– **James Brown**

Never take anything for granted.

– **Benjamin Disraeli**

Certainly the research shows that grateful people are more innovative thinkers.

– **Deborah Norville**

The first thing I do when I start my day is, I get down on my hands and knees and give thanks to God. Whenever I go outside of my house, the first thing I do is stop at the church.

– **Mark Wahlberg**

Many of our prayers were not answered, and for this we are now grateful.

– **William Feather**

I turn to someone, I'm not sure, to God I think, but I never ask for anything. I would never pray to win a title; it makes no sense. I've never understood those who pray before a match. I simply give thanks for what I have received.

- Mario Balotelli

I think my mother is my biggest influence. There are so many things I hate about her but at the same time I'm thankful for her. All I know is that when I'm a parent I want to be just like my mom. I can talk to my mom more than any of my friends could talk to their parents.

- Nikki Reed

I have a lot to be thankful for. I am healthy, happy and I am loved.

- Reba McEntire

If you are really thankful, what do you do? You share.

- W. Clement Stone

The thankful receiver bears a plentiful harvest.

- William Blake

Thanksgiving is a time when the world gets to see just how blessed and how workable the Christian system is. The emphasis is not on giving or buying, but on being thankful and expressing that appreciation to God and to one another.

- John Clayton

When you read a piece of writing that you admire, send a note of thanks to the author.

- Sherman Alexie

Should it happen tomorrow, I would fall to my knees to give thanks to God for such a career.

- Placido Domingo

In everyone's life, at some time, our inner fire goes out. It is then burst into flame by an encounter with another human being. We should all be thankful for those people who rekindle the inner spirit.

- Albert Schweitzer

Talent is God-given; be humble. Fame is man-given; be thankful. Conceit is self-given; be careful.

- Harvey Mackay

Often people ask how I manage to be happy despite having no arms and no legs. The quick answer is that I have a choice. I can be angry about not having limbs, or I can be thankful that I have a purpose. I chose gratitude.

- Nick Vujicic

I'm thankful for every moment.

- Al Green

Strive to find things to be thankful for, and just look for the good in who you are!

- Bethany Hamilton

If a fellow isn't thankful for what he's got, he isn't likely to be thankful for what he's going to get.

- Frank A. Clark

Drink and be thankful to the host! What seems insignificant when you have it, is important when you need it.

- Franz Grillparzer

The only jobs kids have are to do well in school, to be charming and polite, and be thankful. That's it. I'll house you, protect you, I'll even give my life for you, and in return, you will behave.

- Gene Simmons

I learn more with every job, and I'm very thankful for where I am.

- Liam Hemsworth

My advice: Take a second out of the day today and be thankful for your family.

- Jenna Morasca

I think the best advice came from Drew Barrymore, about always finding love in everything you do and keeping a positive attitude and being thankful.

- Bella Thorne

For what I have received may the Lord make me truly thankful. And more truly for what I have not received.

- Storm Jameson

I'm just very thankful. And I say that a lot because that's the most important message.

- Pharrell Williams

He enjoys much who is thankful for little.

- Thomas Secker

I believe that human beings are born first and given passports later. I'm really thankful for my journey. And it's a journey I didn't design.

- Alfonso Cuaron

I realize how unique my path has been. And I'm thankful for that.

- Vanessa Paradis

As a child, I didn't know what I didn't have. I'm thankful for the challenges early on in my life because now I have a perspective on the world and kind of know what's important.

- America Ferrera

In Latino culture, the quinceanera's a big thing - it's when a girl becomes a woman. But I think age is just a number - you become a woman with the responsibilities you take on and the decisions you make. I started realizing that every day is a gift - you have every day to be thankful you're alive.

- Emily Rios

If I'm not working, I have home time with my family, and if I spend that stressing what's going to happen next, then it's a waste. I have a lot to be thankful for.

- Ewen Bremner

My relationship with God is what gives me a moral compass on what decisions to make and that stuff. I'm thankful that I have the people around me that I do, and they remind me each day of who I am and what I stand for.

- Alyson Stoner

I have spent over 60 years bent over a guitar and to know that I wrote 70 compositions that masters have recorded, that makes me feel so good and full, and proud and thankful to the good Lord.

- Jerry Reed

I'm thankful I grew up the way I did. It made me a hard worker and insightful to other people's lives.

- Rachel Roy

I am very thankful that I have lived the life I have lived. I am thankful for my Graves' disease, and I tell people, if I had my whole life to live over, I would have it, because it has really made me into the person that I am.

- Gail Devers

I've done it all. I'm thankful and proud of what I've accomplished in my life. I hope to keep doing it.

- Ralph Stanley

I feel so thankful that I'm able to be a part of something that I love to wake up and run to work every day.

- Alexander Wang

I've had bad jobs. Now I have a good one. I'm thankful.

- Maurice Greene

It feels great to win and I can't be more thankful to the Lord for walking me through every step. God was and is so faithful every time.

- Webb Simpson

I'm thankful I don't have parents that I feel I need to get their attention. They've always been there for me.

- Cierra Ramirez

I've been very fortunate. I feel very thankful. I've been able to come home and do some fun things and make it exciting for people here at home.

- Roger Clemens

At Thanksgiving, I always start at the top of my list and say I'm grateful for friends, family, and good health. Then I get more superficial... like being thankful for my Louboutins.

- Christie Brinkley

<u>Health</u>

The first wealth is health.

- Ralph Waldo Emerson

It is health that is real wealth and not pieces of gold and silver.

- Mahatma Gandhi

Happiness lies first of all in health.

- George William Curtis

There is nothing more important than our good health – that's our principal capital asset.

- Arlen Specter

Take care of your body. It's the only place you have to live.

- Jim Rohn

Health is not valued till sickness comes.

- Thomas Fuller

A healthy outside starts from the inside.

- Robert Urich

The way you think, the way you behave, the way you eat, can influence your life for 30 to 50 years.

- Deepak Chopra

Looking after my health today gives me a better hope for tomorrow.

- Anne Wilson Schaef

The groundwork of all happiness is health.

- Leigh Hunt

It is better to be healthy alone, than to be sick with somebody else.

- Phil McGraw

He who has health, has hope; he who has hope, has everything.

- Thomas Carlyle

Early to bed and early to rise makes a man healthy,
wealthy and wise.

- Benjamin Franklin

Your body hears everything your mind says.

- Naomi Judd

Health is not a condition of matter, but of Mind.

- Mary Baker Eddy

Investing in health will produce enormous benefits.

- Gro Harlem Brundtland

Hearty laughter is a good way to jog internally without
having to go outdoors.

- Norman Cousins

I'm healthy as can be – not an ache or a pain. A lot of my
prayer is thanking the Lord that I am healthy. I pray for
long life and good health.

- Joel Osteen

A person whose mind is quiet and satisfied in God is in the pathway to health.

- **Ellen G. White**

Leave all the afternoon for exercise and recreation, which are as necessary as reading. I will rather say more necessary because health is worth more than learning.

- **Thomas Jefferson**

The truth is that stress doesn't come from your boss, your kids, your spouse, traffic jams, health challenges, or other circumstances. It comes from your thoughts about these circumstances.

- **Andrew Bernstein**

To enjoy the glow of good health, you must exercise.

- **Gene Tunney**

Calm mind brings inner strength and self-confidence, so that's very important for good health.

- **Dali Lama**

Health is the thing that makes you feel that now is the best time of the year.

- **Franklin Pierce Adams**

The only way to keep your health is to eat what you don't want, drink what you don't like and do what you'd rather not.

- **Mark Twain**

Health is the greatest possession.

- **Lao Tzu**

If we could give every individual the right amount of nourishment and exercise, not too little and not too much, we would have found the safest way to health.

- **Hippocrates**

Time and health are two precious assets that we don't recognize and appreciate until they have been depleted.

- **Denis Waitley**

Good health and good sense are two of life's greatest blessings.

- **Publilius Syrus**

Self-esteem is as important to our well being as legs are to a table. It is essential for physical and mental health and for happiness.

- **Louise Hart**

Health is the vital principle of bliss, and exercise, of health.

- James Thomson

Tobacco is the only industry that produces products to make huge profits and at the same time damage the health and kill their consumers.

- Margaret Chan

Family, nature and health all go together.

- Olivia Newton-John

You don't have to be a wreck. You don't have to be sick. One's aim in life should be to die in good health. Just like a candle that burns out.

- Jeanne Moreau

I've always wanted to be in the health and wellness business. I try to encourage people to live a healthy lifestyle.

- Mark Wahlberg

The power of community to create health is far greater than any physician, clinic or hospital.

- Mark Hyman

Prevention is one of the few known ways to reduce demand for health and aged care services.

- **Julie Bishop**

All the money in the world can't buy you back good health.

- **Reba McEntire**

Having good health, being able to breath and be happy, that's one of the most beautiful gifts.

- **Roy Ayers**

Laughter is important, not only because it makes us happy, it also has actual health benefits. And that's because laughter completely engages the body and releases the mind. It connects us to others, and that in itself has a healing effect.

- **Marlo Thomas**

True health infuses positive energy in the mind, body and spirit; it is a main focus in my life.

- **Maximillian Degenerez**

Good humour is the health of the soul, sadness, it's poison.
- **Philip Stanhope, 4th Earl of Chesterfield**

Love is not as important as good health. You cannot be in love if you're not healthy. You can't appreciate it.

- Bryan Cranston

One of the most obvious ways dogs can improve our physical and mental health is via daily walks.

- Andrew Weil

Walking is magic. Can't recommend it highly enough. I read that Plato and Aristotle did much of their brilliant thinking together while ambulating. The movement, the meditation, the health of the blood pumping, and the rhythm of footsteps...this is a primal way to connect with one's deeper self.

- Paula Cole

Lucid dreaming has considerable potential for promoting personal growth and self-development, enhancing self-confidence, improving mental and physical health, facilitating creative problem solving and helping you to progress on the path to self-mastery.

- Stephen LaBerge

Property may be destroyed and money may lose its purchasing power; but character, health, knowledge and good judgement will always be in demand under all conditions.

- Roger Babson

And I believe that the best buy in public health today must be a combination of regular physical exercise and a healthy diet.

- Julie Bishop

As a father, physician and nurse, I have a special place in my heart for children, and I know the brief window of opportunity we have to teach them simple lessons that can lead to a lifetime of good health.

- Richard Carmona

What some call health, if purchased by perpetual anxiety about diet, isn't much better than tedious disease.

- Alexander Pope

Sobriety and health is the greatest thing.

- Jeff Bridges

Eating ice cream and not exercising is great. The downside is your health isn't so good.

- Jeff Bridges

Everyone has their own definition of a healthy lifestyle, and mine has come to mean making health a priority but not an obsession.

- Daphne Oz

Health to the ocean means health for us.

- Sylvia Earle

I have long recognized a link between fitness and mental health and I think we need to encourage young people to take part in sports and team activities because we know it has such positive results.

- Tipper Gore

Great amount of scientific research is there to show that health is better because transcendental meditation deals with consciousness, and consciousness is the basic value of all the physical expressions. The entire creation is the expression of consciousness.

- Maharishi Mahesh Yogi

I go running three times a week - outside in the park, come rain or shine, and I hate every moment of it. I hate everything about it. But I know it's important for health reasons and the reason why I run, in particular, is because my stage work is like cardiovascular work so I don't want to lose my breath on stage.

- Paloma Faith

Water and sanitation has not had the same kind of champion that global health, and even education, have had.

- Jim Yong Kim

I purposely don't talk about money, because people are already skeptical about TV preachers. But I do say that I want you to be blessed. To me, prosperity is having health, having great children, having peace, good relationships. It's not about the money.

- Joel Osteen

In a disordered mind, as in a disordered body, soundness of health is impossible.

- Marcus Tullius Cicero

You end up as you deserve. In old age you must put up with the face, the friends, the health, and the children you have earned.

- Judith Viorst

No company is preferable to bad. We are more apt to catch the vices of others than virtues, as disease is far more contagious than health.

- Charles Caleb Colton

When you start fooling around with drugs, you're hurting your creativity; you're hurting your health. Drugs are death, in one form or another. If they don't kill you, they kill your soul. And if your soul's dead, you've got nothing to offer, anyway.

- Paul Stanley

Medicine sometimes snatches away health, sometimes gives it.

- Ovid

For sleep, riches and health to be truly enjoyed, they must be interrupted.

- Jean Paul

Nothing is more capable of troubling our reason, and consuming our health, than secret notions of jealousy in solitude.

- Aphra Behn

It's bizarre that the produce manager is more important to my children's health than the pediatrician.

- **Meryl Streep**

The awareness that health is dependent upon habits that we control makes us the first generation in history that to a large extent determines its own destiny.

- **Jimmy Carter**

The preservation of health is a duty. Few seem conscious that there is such a thing as physical morality.

- **Herbert Spencer**

My health and my family are the core of my being.

- **Jon Bon Jovi**

Teaching kids about health and fitness is important to me. It's about being fit for life.

- **Jackie Joyner-Kersee**

Without your health, everything else means nothing.

- **Mary J. Blige**

I don't have any health problems, but to keep your health improves your quality of life.

- Mary J. Blige

My main goal is to stay healthy because when you're injured you realise how lucky you are to have your health.

- Maria Sharapova

What, after all, is the object of education? To train the body in health, vigor and grace, so that it may express the emotions in beauty and the mind with accuracy and strength.

- Annie Besant

I was one of those people who put too much emphasis on work and career and material possessions, and it took its toll on all my relationships, on my physical health, my emotional and mental health.

- Tony Shalhoub

I've started to treat my health like a science project.

- Sophia Bush

I really believe that beauty comes from health - sensible eating and exercise.

- **Dita Von Teese**

I learned very early that our health is always impaired by some excess either of food or abstinence, and I never had any physician except myself.

- **Giacomo Casanova**

TV does not care about you or what happens to you. It's downright bad for your health now, and that's not a far-out concept. I think watching the TV news is bad for you. It is bad for your physical health and your mental health.

- **Tom Petty**

Make space in your life, space for health and happiness.

- **Kris Carr**

No matter how old you are, no matter how much you weigh, you can still control the health of your body.

- **Mehmet Oz**

A comfortable house is a great source of happiness. It ranks immediately after health and a good conscience.

- **Sydney Smith**

The more easily digestible and refined the carbohydrates, the greater the effect on our health, weight and well-being.

- Andrew Weil

I am in very good health. I've never felt better.

- Hugh Hefner

Taking care of your mental and physical health is just as important as any career move or responsibility.

- Mireille Guiliano

As I mentioned previously, the tools that allow for optimum health are diet and exercise.

- Bill Toomey

I'm actually tougher on myself as I get older. It's a vicious cycle. The things that are important in life are the things that you can't buy in life: love, health and happiness. I say that, and I believe that, and I try to live that.

- Criss Angel

My hobbies include maintaining my physical and mental health. It's a full-time job. Yoga definitely helps for both of them. I'm a big fan of relaxing and not having a schedule. That's my best way to keep from going crazy.

- Olivia Thirlby

The first draught serveth for health, the second for pleasure, the third for shame, and the fourth for madness.

- Anacharsis

It's never too late to take your heart health seriously and make it a priority.

- Jennie Garth

Your own personal health is your own personal choice, all the way down the line.

- Melissa Etheridge

You can have all the riches and success in the world, but if you don't have your health, you have nothing.

- Steven Adler

I believe that stress is a factor in any bad health.

- Christopher Shays

It's not okay to be fat - not because of the way you look, but because it's unhealthy. I have experienced hormonal problems, bad skin, immense laziness, and back and knee pain. It's not fine to be too fat or too thin! Anything in extremes is wrong. I am afraid of putting on weight because I don't want to develop health problems.

- Sonam Kapoor

You can't take good health for granted.

- Jack Osbourne

I try to make my bed every day for mental health. Coming home to an unmade bed or a room with clothes all over will depress me.

- David Alan Grier

My daily schedule is quite hectic, but I have to put my health first in order to be the best mom and wife I can be.

- Ellen Pompeo

Every time you have a carrot instead of a cookie, every time you go to the gym instead of going to the movies, that's a costly investment in your health. But how much you want to invest is going to depend on how much longer you expect to live in the future, even if you don't make those investments.

- Emily Oster

My motivation has always been health - eating healthy and taking care of myself.

- Gabrielle Reece

I want to encourage everyone to be proactive with their health and get checked out.

- Giuliana Rancic

When you're young, you don't think very far ahead. You just think in terms of the next day, the next week, the next competition. You don't think about injuries that could threaten your long-term health.

- Katarina Witt

Because I would give it all back to have my health.

- David Gest

To get rich never risk your health. For it is the truth that health is the wealth of wealth.

- Richard Baker

Using lots of fresh foods, fruits and vegetables, helps to keep the menu buoyant - I don't know if that's the right word, but it keeps a balance of freshness and health.

- Sally Schneider

It's funny; I do try to maintain health. I started doing Bikram yoga, which is that hothouse yoga, the 105 degrees yoga for 90 minutes. It's great, you purge out all the sweat and you're drinking water.

- Bryan Cranston

The state of the health of the individual is equivalent to the state to the health of the colon.

- Woody Harrelson

We know a great deal more about the causes of physical disease than we do about the causes of physical health.

- M. Scott Peck

Yoga is at the core of my health and wellness routine; even if it's only for 10 to 15 minutes I find it helps me to re-center and to focus as well as improve my overall core strength.

- Miranda Kerr

Apart from education, you need good health, and for that, you need to play sports.

- Kapil Dev

I turned into a workaholic to the point of where my health was in jeopardy.

- **Tab Hunter**

Health is the state about which medicine has nothing to say.

- **W. H. Auden**

I think about my parents all the time, especially on Sunday when I'm at Mass. My mother always said, 'We do not pray to win elections. We pray for people's health, we pray that God's will, be done; we pray that we do our best. But we do not pray to win elections.'

- **Nancy Pelosi**

I'm a health nut, but when I eat, I go hard.

- **Kevin Hart**

I pay a bit more than lip-service to health: I don't eat chips or pre-prepared food, and it might be a comedy sacrilege to admit I do like vegetables, fruit and salad and stuff.

- **Jo Brand**

We drink one another's health and spoil our own.

- **Jerome K. Jerome**

The doctor has been taught to be interested not in health but in disease. What the public is taught is that health is the cure for disease.

- Ashley Montagu

I pray every day, several times. It soothes me. I don't ask for anything, except for health.

- Jon Bon Jovi

Being a vegan is pretty easy these days, as almost every town and city has health food stores and vegetarian-friendly restaurants.

- Moby

Age does not depend upon years, but upon temperament and health. Some men are born old, and some never grow so.

- Tryon Edwards

Just as physical exercise is a well-known and well-accepted means to improve health for anyone, regardless of age or background, so can the brain be put 'into shape' for optimal learning.

- Naveen Jain

I'm 58 years old and I just went through 8 back surgeries. They started cutting on me in February 2009, and I was basically bed ridden for almost two years. I got a real dose of reality that if you don't have your health, you don't have anything.

- **Hulk Hogan**

Yoga is wonderful. It clears up most health problems. It also gives you an overview.

- **Helen Reddy**

Balance is key: I need to be successful in my career to feel fulfilled, be surrounded by people I care about to share it with, and have my health to be able to do the things I love to do!

- **Kiana Tom**

Gut health is the key to overall health.

- **Kris Carr**

I'm nutty for nutrition. I've become one of those people who can't stop talking about the connection between food and health. Now that I know how much changing what you eat can transform your life, I can't stop proselytizing.

- **Robin Quivers**

I try to stay positive by focusing on how much I'll appreciate my health if I get better.

- Daniel Johns

I think health is the outcome of eating well.

- Alice Waters

Obesity affects every aspect of a people's lives, from health to relationships.

- Jane Velez-Mitchell

Oh my gosh, I feel like I'm really obsessive about anything dealing with my health.

- Ginnifer Goodwin

High-quality food is better for your health.

- Michael Pollan

The myriad of serious health risks resulting from poor diet include high cholesterol, heart disease, type 2 diabetes, high blood pressure, stroke, and even sleep apnea.

- Jane Velez-Mitchell

I try to focus on eating seasonally and organic whenever possible. It can be a challenge, but it has a huge effect on my weight, my health, and the environment.

- **Elle Macpherson**

Exercise keeps me occupied, which is good for my mental health.

- **Gail Porter**

In my forties, my optimism was boundless. I had really good health and tremendous success which allowed me to do anything I wanted.

- **Patricia Cornwell**

Of the five most important things in life, health is first, education or knowledge is second, and wealth is third. I forget the other two.

- **Chuck Berry**

When I was on Broadway, I got really sick with walking pneumonia. I decided not to take my health for granted anymore and make it a priority. The great thing is, the pounds just started to fall off.

- **Jordin Sparks**

I have relied on prayer for health care all of my life.

- Henry Paulson

If you can eat 70 percent raw or introduce raw into your diet, it will help your health.

- Carol Alt

Happiness

It is not how much we have, but how much we enjoy, that makes happiness.

- **Charles Spurgeon**

I am determined to be cheerful and happy in whatever situation I may find myself. For I have learned that the greater part of our misery or unhappiness is determined not by our circumstance but by our disposition.

- **Martha Washington**

Be happy for this moment. This moment is your life.

- **Omar Khayyam**

There is only one happiness in this life, to love and be loved.

- **George Sand**

Happiness is not something ready made. It comes from your own actions.

- **Dalai Lama**

Happiness is when what you think, what you say, and what you do are in harmony.

                                        - **Mahatma Gandhi**

Happiness is like a kiss. You must share it to enjoy it.

                                        - **Bernard Meltzer**

Our greatest happiness does not depend on the condition of life in which chance has placed us, but is always the result of a good conscience, good health, occupation, and freedom in all just pursuits.

                                        - **Thomas Jefferson**

Happiness... consists in giving, and in serving others.

                                        - **Henry Drummond**

Most folks are as happy as they make up their minds to be.

                                        - **Abraham Lincoln**

Try to make at least one person happy every day. If you cannot do a kind deed, speak a kind word. If you cannot speak a kind word, think a kind thought. Count up, if you can, the treasure of happiness that you would dispense in a week, in a year, in a lifetime!

                                        - **Lawrence G. Lovasik**

Happiness often sneaks in through a door you didn't know you left open.

- John Barrymore

Remember that the happiest people are not those getting more, but those giving more.

- H. Jackson Brown, Jr.

Happiness depends upon ourselves.

- Aristotle

If you want others to be happy, practice compassion. If you want to be happy, practice compassion.

- Dalai Lama

Nothing brings me more happiness than trying to help the most vulnerable people in society. It is a goal and an essential part of my life - a kind of destiny. Whoever is in distress can call on me. I will come running wherever they are.

- Princess Diana

True happiness... is not attained through self-gratification, but through fidelity to a worthy purpose.

- Helen Keller

Some cause happiness wherever they go; others whenever they go.

- Oscar Wilde

Happiness is dependent on self-discipline. We are the biggest obstacles to our own happiness. It is much easier to do battle with society and with others than to fight our own nature.

- Dennis Prager

The art of being happy lies in the power of extracting happiness from common things.

- Henry Ward Beecher

Everyone chases after happiness, not noticing that happiness is right at their heels.

- Bertolt Brecht

Happy is the man who has broken the chains which hurt the mind, and has given up worrying once and for all.

- Ovid

The moments of happiness we enjoy take us by surprise. It is not that we seize them, but that they seize us.

- Ashley Montagu

Now and then it's good to pause in our pursuit of happiness and just be happy.

- Guillaume Apollinaire

Happiness isn't something you experience; it's something you remember.

- Oscar Levant

It is neither wealth nor splendor; but tranquillity and occupation which give you happiness.

- Thomas Jefferson

There is only one passion, the passion for happiness.

- Denis Diderot

If your happiness depends on what somebody else does, I guess you do have a problem.

- Richard Bach

The person born with a talent they are meant to use will find their greatest happiness in using it.

- Johann Wolfgang von Goethe

A hug is like a boomerang - you get it back right away.

- Bil Keane

Happiness is that state of consciousness which proceeds from the achievement of one's values.

- Ayn Rand

You must try to generate happiness within yourself. If you aren't happy in one place, chances are you won't be happy anyplace.

- Ernie Banks

Plenty of people miss their share of happiness, not because they never found it, but because they didn't stop to enjoy it.

- William Feather

Happiness is the only good. The time to be happy is now. The place to be happy is here. The way to be happy is to make others so.

- Robert Green Ingersoll

The secret of happiness is to admire without desiring.

- Carl Sandburg

The two enemies of human happiness are pain and boredom.

- Arthur Schopenhauer

It's enough to indulge and to be selfish but true happiness is really when you start giving back.

- Adrian Grenier

You know its love when all you want is that person to be happy, even if you're not part of their happiness.

- Julia Roberts

The most worthwhile thing is to try to put happiness into the lives of others.

- Robert Baden-Powell

Research has shown that the best way to be happy is to make each day happy.

- Deepak Chopra

Happiness includes chiefly the idea of satisfaction after full honest effort. No one can possibly be satisfied and no one can be happy who feels that in some paramount affairs he failed to take up the challenge of life.

- Arnold Bennett

When what we are is what we want to be, that's happiness.
                                        - Malcolm Forbes

Happiness comes only when we push our brains and hearts
to the farthest reaches of which we are capable.
                                        - Leo Rosten

Every gift from a friend is a wish for your happiness.
                                        - Richard Bach

Do not speak of your happiness to one less fortunate than
yourself.
                                        - Plutarch

Your successes and happiness are forgiven you only if you
generously consent to share them.
                                        - Albert Camus

In times of joy, all of us wished we possessed a tail we
could wag.
                                        - W. H. Auden

Money can't buy you happiness, but it can buy you a yacht big enough to pull up right alongside it.

- David Lee Roth

Happiness is not a goal; it is a by-product.

- Eleanor Roosevelt

Desire nothing, give up all desires and be happy.

- Swami Sivananda

That should be the measure of success for everyone. It's not money, it's not fame, it's not celebrity; my index of success is happiness.

- Lupe Fiasco

Happiness? A good cigar, a good meal, a good cigar and a good woman - or a bad woman; it depends on how much happiness you can handle.

- George Burns

Don't wait around for other people to be happy for you. Any happiness you get you've got to make yourself.

- Alice Walker

Action may not always bring happiness; but there is no happiness without action.

- Benjamin Disraeli

If you hope for happiness in the world, hope for it from God, and not from the world.

- David Brainerd

You've got to ask! Asking is, in my opinion, the world's most powerful - and neglected - secret to success and happiness.

- Percy Ross

All happiness or unhappiness solely depends upon the quality of the object to which we are attached by love.

- Baruch Spinoza

Happy he who learns to bear what he cannot change.

- Friedrich Schiller

Love is the most terrible, and also the most generous of the passions; it is the only one which includes in its dreams the happiness of someone else.

- Alphonse Karr

You can be happy where you are.

- Joel Osteen

Happiness is no laughing matter.

- Richard Whately

Happiness is an inside job.

- William Arthur Ward

Happiness is good health and a bad memory.

- Ingrid Bergman

Happiness is itself a kind of gratitude.

- Joseph Wood Krutch

Happiness is a virtue, not its reward.

- Baruch Spinoza

When ambition ends, happiness begins.

- Thomas Merton

What we call the secret of happiness is no more a secret than our willingness to choose life.

- Leo Buscaglia

Happiness is mostly a by-product of doing what makes us feel fulfilled.

- Benjamin Spock

To forget oneself is to be happy.

- Robert Louis Stevenson

There is something curiously boring about somebody else's happiness.

- Aldous Huxley

Happiness is a continuation of happenings, which are not resisted.

- Deepak Chopra

The secret of happiness is something to do.

- John Burroughs

To buy happiness is to sell soul.

- Douglas Horton

Happiness is a by-product. You cannot pursue it by itself.

- **Sam Levenson**

If you have easy self-contentment, you might have a very, very cheap source of happiness.

- **Leon Kass**

Happiness never lays its finger on its pulse.

- **Adam Smith**

Desire is individual. Happiness is common.

- **Julian Casablancas**

Always leave something to wish for; otherwise you will be miserable from your very happiness.

- **Baltasar Gracian**

It's pretty hard to tell what does bring happiness; poverty and wealth have both failed.

- **Kin Hubbard**

A sure way to lose happiness, I found, is to want it at the expense of everything else.

- **Bette Davis**

Never mind your happiness; do your duty.

- Peter Drucker

If you wait for the perfect moment when all is safe and assured, it may never arrive. Mountains will not be climbed, races won, or lasting happiness achieved.

- Maurice Chevalier

Growth itself contains the germ of happiness.

- Pearl S. Buck

Happiness is found in doing, not merely possessing.

- Napoleon Hill

For happiness one needs security, but joy can spring like a flower even from the cliffs of despair.

- Anne Morrow Lindbergh

People let their own hang-ups become the obstacles between them and personal happiness.

- Lucinda Williams

Most of us believe in trying to make other people happy only if they can be happy in ways, which we approve.

- Robert Staughton Lynd

Eternal principles that govern happiness apply equally to all.

- Russell M. Nelson

The action is best that secures the greatest happiness for the greatest number.

- William Dean Howells

We possess only the happiness we are able to understand.

- Maurice Maeterlinck

There is happiness in duty, although it may not seem so.

- Jose Marti

Only man clogs his happiness with care, destroying what is with thoughts of what may be.

- John Dryden

Happiness is composed of misfortunes avoided.

- Alphonse Karr

Happiness is the interval between periods of unhappiness.

- Don Marquis

Happiness: an agreeable sensation arising from contemplating the misery of another.

- Ambrose Bierce

Anything you're good at contributes to happiness.

- Bertrand Russell

Life everlasting in a state of happiness is the greatest desire of all men.

- Joseph Franklin Rutherford

Happiness depends more on how life strikes you than on what happens.

- Andy Rooney

Happiness does not consist in self-love.

- Joseph Butler

The right to happiness is fundamental.

- Anna Pavlova

Love is when the other person's happiness is more important than your own.

- H. Jackson Brown, Jr.

Friends show their love in times of trouble, not in happiness.

- Euripides

You will never be happy if you continue to search for what happiness consists of. You will never live if you are looking for the meaning of life.

- Albert Camus

We hold these truths to be self-evident: that all men are created equal; that they are endowed by their Creator with certain unalienable rights; that among these are life, liberty, and the pursuit of happiness.

- Thomas Jefferson

Happiness lies in the joy of achievement and the thrill of creative effort.

- Franklin D. Roosevelt

A smile is happiness you'll find right under your nose.

- Tom Wilson

Happiness, true happiness, is an inner quality. It is a state of mind. If your mind is at peace, you are happy. If your mind is at peace, but you have nothing else, you can be happy. If you have everything the world can give - pleasure, possessions, power - but lack peace of mind, you can never be happy.

- Dada Vaswani

Every day is a new day, and you'll never be able to find happiness if you don't move on.

- Carrie Underwood

Your success and happiness lies in you. Resolve to keep happy, and your joy and you shall form an invincible host against difficulties.

- Helen Keller

Christmas is the spirit of giving without a thought of getting. It is happiness because we see joy in people. It is forgetting self and finding time for others. It is discarding the meaningless and stressing the true values.

- Thomas S. Monson

Success is getting what you want. Happiness is wanting what you get.

- Dale Carnegie

Thousands of candles can be lighted from a single candle, and the life of the candle will not be shortened. Happiness never decreases by being shared.

- Buddha

So long as we can lose any happiness, we possess some.

- Booth Tarkington

The true secret of happiness lies in taking a genuine interest in all the details of daily life.

- William Morris

To enjoy good health, to bring true happiness to one's family, to bring peace to all, one must first discipline and control one's own mind. If a man can control his mind he can find the way to Enlightenment, and all wisdom and virtue will naturally come to him.

- Buddha

Happiness resides not in possessions, and not in gold, happiness dwells in the soul.

- Democritus

Every day we have plenty of opportunities to get angry, stressed or offended. But what you're doing when you indulge these negative emotions is giving something outside yourself power over your happiness. You can choose to not let little things upset you.

- Joel Osteen

The word 'happiness' would lose its meaning if it were not balanced by sadness.

- Carl Jung

Some days are just bad days, that's all. You have to experience sadness to know happiness, and I remind myself that not every day is going to be a good day, that's just the way it is!

- Dita Von Teese

In this life, we have to make many choices. Some are very important choices. Some are not. Many of our choices are between good and evil. The choices we make, however, determine to a large extent our happiness or our unhappiness, because we have to live with the consequences of our choices.

- James E. Faust

My greatest beauty secret is being happy with myself. I don't use special creams or treatments - I'll use a little bit of everything. It's a mistake to think you are what you put on yourself. I believe that a lot of how you look is to do with how you feel about yourself and your life. Happiness is the greatest beauty secret.

- Tina Turner

True happiness involves the full use of one's power and talents.

- John W. Gardner

The happiness of life is made up of minute fractions - the little, soon forgotten charities of a kiss or a smile, a kind look or heartfelt compliment.

- Samuel Taylor Coleridge

The man who makes everything that leads to happiness depends upon himself, and not upon other men, has adopted the very best plan for living happily. This is the man of moderation, the man of manly character and of wisdom.

- Plato

Happiness is not something you postpone for the future; it is something you design for the present.

- Jim Rohn

Morality is not the doctrine of how we may make ourselves happy, but how we may make ourselves worthy of happiness.

- **Immanuel Kant**

I think most of us are raised with preconceived notions of the choices we're supposed to make. We waste so much time making decisions based on someone else's idea of our happiness - what will make you a good citizen or a good wife or daughter or actress. Nobody says, 'Just be happy - go be a cobbler or go live with goats.'

- **Sandra Bullock**

You take away all the other luxuries in life, and if you can make someone smile and laugh, you have given the most special gift: happiness.

- **Brad Garrett**

Money won't buy happiness, but it will pay the salaries of a large research staff to study the problem.

- **Bill Vaughan**

Happiness does not come from doing easy work but from the afterglow of satisfaction that comes after the achievement of a difficult task that demanded our best.

- **Theodore Isaac Rubin**

Three grand essentials to happiness in this life are something to do, something to love, and something to hope for.

- **Joseph Addison**

Happiness is a choice. You can choose to be happy. There's going to be stress in life, but it's your choice whether you let it affect you or not.

- **Valerie Bertinelli**

It is very important to generate a good attitude, a good heart, as much as possible. From this, happiness in both the short term and the long term for both yourself and others will come.

- **Dalai Lama**

Happiness held is the seed; Happiness shared is the flower.

- **John Harrigan**

Problems or successes, they all are the results of our own actions. Karma. The philosophy of action is that no one else is the giver of peace or happiness. One's own karma, one's own actions are responsible to come to bring either happiness or success or whatever.

- **Maharishi Mahesh Yogi**

Happiness is only real when shared.
                                    - **Christopher McCandless**

The most simple things can bring the most happiness.
                                    - **Izabella Scorupco**

Crying is cleansing. There's a reason for tears, happiness or sadness.
                                    - **Dionne Warwick**

The greatest happiness of life is the conviction that we are loved; loved for ourselves, or rather, loved in spite of ourselves.
                                    - **Victor Hugo**

I think happiness is a choice. If you feel yourself being happy and can settle in to the life choices you make, then it's great. It's really, really great. I swear to God, happiness is the best makeup.
                                    - **Drew Barrymore**

Happiness radiates like the fragrance from a flower and draws all good things towards you.
                                    - **Maharishi Mahesh Yogi**

One thing I didn't understand in life was that I had $100,000,000 in the bank and I couldn't buy happiness. I had everything: mansions, yachts, Ferraris, Lamborghinis, but I was depressed. I didn't know where I fitted in. But then I found family and friends and I learned the value of life.

- Vanilla Ice

Caring about others, running the risk of feeling, and leaving an impact on people, brings happiness.

- Harold Kushner

My happiness doesn't come from money or fame. My happiness comes from seeing life without struggle.

- Nicki Minaj

True happiness arises, in the first place, from the enjoyment of one's self, and in the next, from the friendship and conversation of a few select companions.

- Joseph Addison

Most of us need time to work through pain and loss. We can find all manner of reasons for postponing forgiveness. One of these reasons is waiting for the wrongdoers to repent before we forgive them. Yet such a delay causes us to forfeit the peace and happiness that could be ours.

- James E. Faust

Being happy is of the utmost importance. Success in anything is through happiness.

- **Maharishi Mahesh Yogi**

There is joy in work. There is no happiness except in the realization that we have accomplished something.

- **Henry Ford**

Life is full of happiness and tears; be strong and have faith.

- **Kareena Kapoor Khan**

Success is not the key to happiness. Happiness is the key to success. If you love what you are doing, you will be successful.

- **Albert Schweitzer**

There is no fulfilment in things whatsoever. And I think one of the reasons that depression reigns supreme amongst the rich and famous is some of them thought that maybe those things would bring them happiness. But what, in fact, does is having a cause, having a passion. And that's really what gives life's true meaning.

- **Benjamin Carson**

Procrastination is one of the most common and deadliest of diseases and its toll on success and happiness is heavy.

- Wayne Gretzky

We are buried beneath the weight of information, which is being confused with knowledge; quantity is being confused with abundance and wealth with happiness.

- Tom Waits

You might not make it to the top, but if you are doing what you love, there is much more happiness there than being rich or famous.

- Tony Hawk

The world is full of a lot of fear and a lot of negativity, and a lot of judgment. I just think people need to start shifting into joy and happiness. As corny as it sounds, we need to make a shift.

- Ellen DeGeneres

I enjoy being happy every day, and hopefully you can hear my happiness in my music. Life is beautiful.

- Christina Milian

True happiness arises, in the first place, from the enjoyment of one's self, and in the next, from the friendship and conversation of a few select companions.

- Joseph Addison

Man is fond of counting his troubles, but he does not count his joys. If he counted them up as he ought to, he would see that every lot has enough happiness provided for it.

- Fyodor Dostoevsky

I don't have to chase extraordinary moments to find happiness - it's right in front of me if I'm paying attention and practicing gratitude.

- Brene Brown

The greatest of follies is to sacrifice health for any other kind of happiness.

- Arthur Schopenhauer

Understanding your employee's perspective can go a long way towards increasing productivity and happiness.

- Kathryn Minshew

There is no value in life except what you choose to place upon it and no happiness in any place except what you bring to it yourself.

- **Henry David Thoreau**

In my life I've learned that true happiness comes from giving. Helping others along the way makes you evaluate who you are. I think that love is what we're all searching for. I haven't come across anyone who didn't become a better person through love.

- **Marla Gibbs**

There is no cosmetic for beauty like happiness.

- **Maria Mitchell**

Beauty is the promise of happiness.

- **Edmund Burke**

My happiness grows in direct proportion to my acceptance, and in inverse proportion to my expectations.

- **Michael J. Fox**

It is not in the pursuit of happiness that we find fulfilment; it is in the happiness of pursuit.

- **Denis Waitley**

It is the ultimate luxury to combine passion and contribution. It's also a very clear path to happiness.

- Sheryl Sandberg

Joy can only be real if people look upon their life as a service and have a definite object in life outside themselves and their personal happiness.

- Leo Tolstoy

I would maintain that thanks are the highest form of thought, and that gratitude is happiness doubled by wonder.

- Gilbert K. Chesterton

The folly of endless consumerism sends us on a wild goose-chase for happiness through materialism.

- Bryant H. McGill

The greatest happiness is to know the source of unhappiness.

- Fyodor Dostoevsky

Our daily decisions and habits have a huge impact upon both our levels of happiness and success.

- Shawn Achor

The foundation of success in life is good health: that is the substratum fortune; it is also the basis of happiness. A person cannot accumulate a fortune very well when he is sick.

- **P. T. Barnum**

The greater part of our happiness or misery depends on our dispositions and not our circumstances.

- **Martha Washington**

Happiness and moral duty are inseparably connected.

- **George Washington**

A man who as a physical being is always turned toward the outside, thinking that his happiness lies outside him, finally turns inward and discovers that the source is within him.

- **Soren Kierkegaard**

There is a difference between happiness and wisdom: he that thinks himself the happiest man is really so; but he that thinks himself the wisest is generally the greatest fool.

- **Francis Bacon**

A mother's happiness is like a beacon, lighting up the future but reflected also on the past in the guise of fond memories.

— **Honore de Balzac**

Imagination disposes of everything; it creates beauty, justice, and happiness, which are everything in this world.

— **Blaise Pascal**

I think essentially the meaning of life is probably the journey and not really any one thing or an outcome or a result. I think it's kinda the process and I think that if you can find happiness in the process then maybe that's it.

— **Charisma Carpenter**

It's part of life to have obstacles. It's about overcoming obstacles; that's the key to happiness.

— **Herbie Hancock**

Live by this credo: have a little laugh at life and look around you for happiness instead of sadness. Laughter has always brought me out of unhappy situations.

— **Red Skelton**

Being of service to others is what brings true happiness.

- **Marie Osmond**

Since you get more joy out of giving joy to others, you should put a good deal of thought into the happiness that you are able to give.

- **Eleanor Roosevelt**

No one is perfect... absolutely no one. Like precious stones, we have a few flaws, but why focus on that? Focus on what you like about yourself, and that will bring you happiness and peace.

- **Richard Simmons**

I've never felt like I was in the cookie business. I've always been in a feel good feeling business. My job is to sell joy. My job is to sell happiness. My job is to sell an experience.

- **Debbi Fields**

Making money is a happiness. And that's a great incentive. Making other people happy is a super-happiness.

- **Muhammad Yunus**

The happiness of one's own heart alone cannot satisfy the soul; one must try to include, as necessary to one's own happiness, the happiness of others.

— **Paramahansa Yogananda**

The groundwork of all happiness is health.

— **Leigh Hunt**

When you're happy you find pure joy in your life. There are no regrets in this state of happiness - and that's a goal worth striving for in all areas of your life.

— **Suze Orman**

One of the first conditions of happiness is that the link between Man and Nature shall not be broken.

— **Leo Tolstoy**

A man is not rightly conditioned until he is a happy, healthy, and prosperous being; and happiness, health, and prosperity are the result of a harmonious adjustment of the inner with the outer of the man with his surroundings.

— **James Allen**

There is no way to happiness - happiness is the way.

— **Thich Nhat Hanh**

Are you bored with life? Then throw yourself into some work you believe in with all your heart, live for it, die for it, and you will find happiness that you had thought could never be yours.

- **Dale Carnegie**

Travelling is the ruin of all happiness! There's no looking at a building after seeing Italy.

- **Fanny Burney**

Happiness is within. It has nothing to do with how much applause you get or how many people praise you. Happiness comes when you believe that you have done something truly meaningful.

- **Martin Yan**

I am a spiritual person in an eastern religion kind of way. I learned that happiness for all of us is a switch that you flick in your brain. It doesn't have anything to do with getting a new house, a new car, a new girlfriend, or a new pair of shoes. Our culture is very much about that; we are never happy with what we have today.

- **Tom Ford**

Well, there are two kinds of happiness, grounded and ungrounded. Ungrounded happiness is cheesy and not based on reality. Grounded happiness is informed happiness based on the knowledge that the world sometimes sucks, but even then you have to believe in yourself.

- Andy Grammer

The happiness and peace attained by those satisfied by the nectar of spiritual tranquillity is not attained by greedy persons restlessly moving here and there.

- Chanakya

There are terrible jerks, and there are an unusually large concentration of them in the workplace. And that means that you do have to make some changes in your behavior, but there is absolutely no need for you to give them power over your happiness.

- Srikumar Rao

Happiness is your own treasure because it lies within you.

- Prem Rawat

Many persons have a wrong idea of what constitutes true happiness. It is not attained through self-gratification but through fidelity to a worthy purpose.

- Helen Keller

Success is getting and achieving what you want. Happiness is wanting and being content with what you get.

- Bernard Meltzer

It is one of my sources of happiness never to desire a knowledge of other people's business.

- Dolley Madison

Happiness is a thing to be practiced, like the violin.

- John Lubbock

One test of the correctness of educational procedure is the happiness of the child.

- Maria Montessori

Happiness is neither virtue nor pleasure nor this thing nor that but simply growth, We are happy when we are growing.

- William Butler Yeats

More compassionate mind, more sense of concern for other's well-being, is source of happiness.

- Dalai Lama

Genuine happiness can only be achieved when we transform our way of life from the unthinking pursuit of pleasure to one committed to enriching our inner lives, when we focus on 'being more' rather than simply having more.

- Daisaku Ikeda

I'm fulfilled in what I do. I never thought that a lot of money or fine clothes - the finer things of life - would make you happy. My concept of happiness is to be filled in a spiritual sense.

- Coretta Scott King

Life's greatest happiness is to be convinced we are loved.

- Victor Hugo

Mindfulness helps you go home to the present. And every time you go there and recognize a condition of happiness that you have, happiness comes.

- Thich Nhat Hanh

A good education is another name for happiness.

- Ann Plato

The pursuit of happiness is a most ridiculous phrase: if you pursue happiness you'll never find it.

- Carrie Snow

Family and friendships are two of the greatest facilitators of happiness.

- John C. Maxwell

I have discovered the secret of happiness - it is work, either with the hands or the head. The moment I have something to do, the draughts are open and my chimney draws, and I am happy.

- John Burroughs

There is no such thing as the pursuit of happiness, but there is the discovery of joy.

- Joyce Grenfell

Wealth, like happiness, is never attained when sought after directly. It comes as a by-product of providing a useful service.

- Henry Ford

Happiness is an attitude of mind, born of the simple determination to be happy under all outward circumstances.

- J. Donald Walters

The secret of happiness is: Find something more important than you are and dedicate your life to it.

- Daniel Dennett

Happiness consists in activity. It is a running steam, not a stagnant pool.

- John Mason Good

I am more and more convinced that our happiness or our unhappiness depends far more on the way we meet the events of life than on the nature of those events themselves.

- Wilhelm von Humboldt

The secret of happiness is this: let your interests be as wide as possible, and let your reactions to the things and persons that interest you be as far as possible friendly rather than hostile.

- Bertrand Russell

People look to time in expectation that it will eventually make them happy, but you cannot find true happiness by looking toward the future.

- Eckhart Tolle

Social scientists have found that the fastest way to feel happiness is to practice gratitude.

- Chip Conley

Success in its highest and noblest form calls for peace of mind and enjoyment and happiness which come only to the man who has found the work that he likes best.

- Napoleon Hill

There is nothing I fear more than waking up without a program that will help me bring a little happiness to those with no resources, those who are poor, illiterate, and ridden with terminal disease.

- Nelson Mandela

Happiness is a how; not a what. A talent, not an object.

Hermann Hesse

I have learned to seek my happiness by limiting my desires, rather than in attempting to satisfy them.

- John Stuart Mill

You may get an emotional thrill when you first buy something, but emotions are fickle. You buy that one thing you think will complete your happiness, but after awhile the feeling goes away and you have to go to the next thing. You just keep going from purchase to purchase looking for the one thing that will finally satisfy. But stuff can't satisfy.

- Joyce Meyer

Happiness is very simple and minimal.

- Tablo

We all want to help one another. Human beings are like that. We want to live by each other's happiness, not by each other's misery.

- Charlie Chaplin

The essence of philosophy is that a man should so live that his happiness shall depend as little as possible on external things.

- Epictetus

I don't have to take a trip around the world or be on a yacht in the Mediterranean to have happiness. I can find it in the little things, like looking out into my backyard and seeing deer in the fields.

- **Queen Latifah**

Remember happiness doesn't depend upon who you are or what you have; it depends solely on what you think.

- **Dale Carnegie**

When you're passionate about something, you want it to be all it can be. But in the endgame of life, I fundamentally believe the key to happiness is letting go of that idea of perfection.

- **Debra Messing**

Happiness for me is totally just being at peace knowing that, everything I'm doing, God is pleased with that. It's complete peace for me.

- **Tyler Perry**

Work and live to serve others, to leave the world a little better than you found it and garner for yourself as much peace of mind as you can. This is happiness.

- **David Sarnoff**

True success, true happiness lies in freedom and fulfilment.

- **Dada Vaswani**

No one is in control of your happiness but you; therefore, you have the power to change anything about yourself or your life that you want to change.

- **Barbara de Angelis**

Happiness comes of the capacity to feel deeply, to enjoy simply, to think freely, to risk life, to be needed.

- **Storm Jameson**

Everyone has their own way of expressing happiness.

- **Shahrukh Khan**

Money is human happiness in the abstract; he, then, who is no longer capable of enjoying human happiness in the concrete, devotes himself utterly to money.

- **Arthur Schopenhauer**

People take different roads seeking fulfilment and happiness. Just because they're not on your road doesn't mean they've gotten lost.

- **H. Jackson Brown, Jr.**

Happiness always looks small while you hold it in your hands, but let it go, and you learn at once how big and precious it is.

- Maxim Gorky

Money can't buy you happiness but it does bring you a more pleasant form of misery.

- Spike Milligan

I'm living the exact life I planned on living when I was five. My life has taken some turns and changes that I didn't anticipate, and it has brought me different things. I thought material things would bring me happiness, which they didn't. But through this, I have learned what things are important and what aren't.

- Tom Ford

The happiness of this life depends less on what befalls you than the way in which you take it.

- Elbert Hubbard

Wealth, like happiness, is never attained when sought after directly. It comes as a by-product of providing a useful service.

- Henry Ford

I discovered that joy is not the negation of pain, but rather acknowledging the presence of pain and feeling happiness in spite of it.

- Lupita Nyong'o

He who has so little knowledge of human nature as to seek happiness by changing anything but his own disposition will waste his life in fruitless efforts.

- Samuel Johnson

No one is in control of your happiness but you; therefore, you have the power to change anything about yourself or your life that you want to change.

- Barbara de Angelis

Contempt for happiness is usually contempt for other people's happiness, and is an elegant disguise for hatred of the human race.

- Bertrand Russell

Mindfulness helps you go home to the present. And every time you go there and recognize a condition of happiness that you have, happiness comes.

- Thich Nhat Hanh

Off with you! You're a happy fellow, for you'll give happiness and joy to many other people. There is nothing better or greater than that!

- Ludwig van Beethoven

Happiness lies first of all in health.

- George William Curtis

Men can only be happy when they do not assume that the object of life is happiness.

- George Orwell

Be more dedicated to making solid achievements than in running after swift but synthetic happiness.

- A. P. J. Abdul Kalam

When we recall the past, we usually find that it is the simplest things - not the great occasions - that in retrospect give off the greatest glow of happiness.

- Bob Hope

Money can't buy happiness.

- Howard Hughe

There is no happiness for people at the expense of other people.

- **Anwar Sadat**

The thing we're all looking for is happiness, and if we achieve just a modicum of that or even a little piece of serenity even for five minutes a day, we're very lucky.

- **Mel Gibson**

Life finds its purpose and fulfilment in the expansion of happiness.

- **Maharishi Mahesh Yogi**

False happiness renders men stern and proud, and that happiness is never communicated. True happiness renders them kind and sensible, and that happiness is always shared.

- **Charles de Montesquieu**

Kind words produce happiness. How often have we ourselves been made happy by kind words, in a manner and to an extent, which we are unable to explain!

- **Frederick William Faber**

Even if happiness forgets you a little bit, never completely forget about it.

- **Jacques Prevert**

I'm a very positive person. My grandmother taught me that happiness is both a skill and a decision, and you are responsible for the outcome.

- **Helen McCrory**

Indeed, man wishes to be happy even when he so lives as to make happiness impossible.

- **Saint Augustine**

Life is to be fortified by many friendships. To love and to be loved is the greatest happiness of existence.

- **Sydney Smith**

Happiness is inward, and not outward; and so, it does not depend on what we have, but on what we are.

- **Henry Van Dyke**

How to gain, how to keep, how to recover happiness is in fact for most men at all times the secret motive of all they do, and of all they are willing to endure.

- **William James**

I always was a rich person because money's not related to happiness.

- Paulo Coelho

Happiness is the reward we get for living to the highest right we know.

- Richard Bach

Happiness is secured through virtue; it is a good attained by man's own will.

- Thomas Aquinas

You believe happiness to be derived from the place in which once you have been happy, but in truth it is centered in ourselves.

- Franz Schubert

It is possible to live happily in the here and the now. So many conditions of happiness are available - more than enough for you to be happy right now. You don't have to run into the future in order to get more.

- Thich Nhat Hanh

God dislikes evil, and no happiness can be built on hate.
Love one another as brothers.

- Josephine Baker

An act of goodness is of itself an act of happiness. No
reward coming after the event can compare with the sweet
reward that went with it.

- Maurice Maeterlinck

The gratification of desire is not happiness.

- Daisaku Ikeda

When you relinquish the desire to control your future, you
can have more happiness.

- Nicole Kidman

Happiness doesn't depend on how much you have to enjoy,
but how much you enjoy what you have.

- Tom Wilson

He who avoids complaint invites happiness.

- Abu Bakr

The most important thing in anyone's life is to be giving something. The quality I can give is fun and joy and happiness. This is my gift.

- **Ginger Rogers**

When I get on stage, my first goal is not to show my expertise, but on the contrary, to give a bit of happiness, of joy, of cheerfulness. I am firmly convinced that in order to sing well, you must love your neighbor and be passionate about life.

- **Andrea Bocelli**

When 'happiness' eludes us - as, eventually, it always will - we have the invitation to examine our programmed responses and to exercise our power to choose again.

- **Richard Rohr**

The single most important factor in our long-term happiness is the relationships we have with our family and close friends.

- **Clayton M. Christensen**

Once you are satisfied with your goal, it is the real happiness.

- **Saina Nehwal**

The mindset of chasing that next #1 record doesn't exist for me anymore. It's more about being a well-rounded entertainer than being a pop artist. Obviously, it would be wonderful to have a hit record but I don't base my happiness on that anymore. It's about the accomplishment of a project that satisfies me. I just want to enjoy the ride.

- Donny Osmond

Happiness comes from... some curious adjustment to life.

- Hugh Walpole

I would hope my legacy would be bringing smiles to faces. Happiness with my music.

- Janet Jackson

Scientifically, happiness is a choice. It is a choice about where your single processor brain will devote its finite resources as you process the world.

- Shawn Achor

Life took over 4 billion years to evolve into you, and you've about 70 more years to enjoy it. Don't just pursue happiness, catch it.

- Eric Idle

I just hope I can spread some of the happiness that's been coming my way.

- **Kenny Rogers**

Chaos is the first condition. Order is the first law. Continuity is the first reflection. Quietude is the first happiness.

- **James Stephens**

That action is best which procures the greatest happiness for the greatest numbers.

- **Francis Hutcheson**

Happiness is the bomb cosmetic! When I'm smiling, sometimes I'm giving thanks for all the things I have rather than worrying about the things I don't.

- **Yaya DaCosta**

We find delight in the beauty and happiness of children that makes the heart too big for the body.

- **Ralph Waldo Emerson**

Of course, to have money is just great because you can do what you think is important to you. I always was a rich person because money's not related to happiness.

- Paulo Coelho

The person who seeks all their applause from outside has their happiness in another's keeping .

- Dale Carnegie

If all our happiness is bound up entirely in our personal circumstances it is difficult not to demand of life more than it has to give.

- Bertrand Russell

I think happiness is a combination of pleasure, engagement and meaningfulness.

- Ian K. Smith

No one has a right to consume happiness without producing it.

- Helen Keller

Happiness is a ball after which we run wherever it rolls, and we push it with our feet when it stops.

- Johann Wolfgang von Goethe

Man needs, for his happiness, not only the enjoyment of this or that, but hope and enterprise and change.

- Bertrand Russell

The supreme happiness of life is the conviction that we are loved; loved for ourselves, or rather in spite of ourselves.

- Victor Hugo

No matter how dull, or how mean, or how wise a man is, he feels that happiness is his indisputable right.

- Helen Keller

But O, how bitter a thing it is to look into happiness through another man's eyes.

- William Shakespeare

Happiness is a mystery, like religion, and should never be rationalised.

- Gilbert K. Chesterton

Even in the common affairs of life, in love, friendship, and marriage, how little security have we when we trust our happiness in the hands of others!

- William Hazlitt

You traverse the world in search of happiness, which is within the reach of every man. A contented mind confers it on all.

- **Horace**

Some of us might find happiness if we quit struggling so desperately for it.

- **William Feather**

The universe is conspiring in every moment to bring me happiness and peace.

- **Marianne Williamson**

While we are focusing on fear, worry, or hate, it is not possible for us to be experiencing happiness, enthusiasm or love.

- **Bo Bennett**

Happiness is a choice that requires effort at times.

- **Aeschylus**

Nothing flatters a man as much as the happiness of his wife; he is always proud of himself as the source of it.

- **Samuel Johnson**

In friendship as well as love, ignorance very often contributes more to our happiness than knowledge.

- Francois de La Rochefoucauld

Happiness is different from pleasure. Happiness has something to do with struggling and enduring and accomplishing.

- George A. Sheehan

If you ever find happiness by hunting for it, you will find it, as the old woman did her lost spectacles, safe on her own nose all the time.

- Josh Billings

Happiness in the present is only shattered by comparison with the past.

- Douglas Horton

God's children and their happiness are my reasons for being.

- Red Skelton

Real happiness is cheap enough, yet how dearly we pay for its counterfeit.

- Hosea Ballou

There is this difference between happiness and wisdom: he that thinks himself the happiest man, really is so; but he that thinks himself the wisest, is generally the greatest fool.

- Charles Caleb Colton

One of the indictments of civilizations is that happiness and intelligence are so rarely found in the same person.

- William Feather

So, my happiness doesn't come from money or fame. My happiness comes from seeing life without struggle.

- Nicki Minaj

Years of happiness can be lost in the foolish gratification of a momentary desire for pleasure.

- Ezra Taft Benson

People are pursuing happiness, but they're pursuing things that will never, ever make them happy, and they don't know that. They've got a distorted view of what will make them happy, what happiness is, and it's based on what they see on television.

- Rush Limbaugh

One of the standards on which your happiness is based, now and in your future, is moral purity.

- **Ezra Taft Benson**

Happiness comes when we test our skills towards some meaningful purpose.

- **John Stossel**

My mother was a public school teacher in Virginia, and we didn't have any money, we just survived on happiness, on being a happy family.

- **Dave Grohl**

Objects we ardently pursue bring little happiness when gained; most of our pleasures come from unexpected sources.

- **Herbert Spencer**

Just stop for a minute and you'll realize you're happy just being. I think it's the pursuit that screws up happiness. If we drop the pursuit, it's right here.

- **James Hillman**

If you really want to receive joy and happiness, then serve others with all your heart. Lift their burden, and your own burden will be lighter.

- Ezra Taft Benson

The most exciting happiness is the happiness generated by forces beyond your control.

- Ogden Nash

There can be no happiness if the things we believe in are different from the things we do.

- Freya Stark

Happiness is understanding that friendship is more precious than mere things, more precious than getting your own way, more precious than being in situations where true principles are not at stake.

- J. Donald Walters

The secret of happiness is the determination to be happy always, rather than wait for outer circumstances to make one happy.

- J. Donald Walters

Most people ask for happiness on condition. Happiness can only be felt if you don't set any condition.

- Arthur Rubinstein

Happiness is not a state to arrive at, but a manner of travelling.

- Margaret Lee Runbeck

I wish people could achieve what they think would bring them happiness in order for them to realize that that's not really what happiness is.

- Alanis Morissette

You know that your happiness and suffering depend on the happiness and suffering of others. That insight helps you not to do wrong things that will bring suffering to yourself and to other people.

- Thich Nhat Hanh

People will survive, and they will find happiness.
Happiness only comes when you're not looking for it.

- Hugh Laurie

Life should be blissful, and blissful doesn't mean just a small happiness. It's huge. It is profound.

- David Lynch

Seek happiness for its own sake, and you will not find it; seek for duty, and happiness will follow as the shadow comes with the sunshine.

- Tryon Edwards

True religion ... is giving and finding one's happiness by bringing happiness into the lives of others.

- William J. H. Boetcker

It's horrible when people are only interested in buying labels, because it doesn't bring them the happiness they think it will.

- Miuccia Prada

The greatest happiness is to transform one's feelings into action.

- Madame de Stael

There is no correlation between happiness and amounts of money.

- Kesha

We've all met those who seem to radiate happiness. They seem to smile more than others; they laugh more than others - just being around them makes us happier as well.

- Joseph B. Wirthlin

People are chasing cash, not happiness. When you chase money, you're going to lose. You're just going to. Even if you get the money, you're not going to be happy.

- Gary Vaynerchuk

Happiness is not a possession to be prized; it is a quality of thought, a state of mind.

- Daphne du Maurier

Happiness comes from the full understanding of your own being.

- Marina Abramovic

I have found that the only thing that does bring you happiness is doing something good for somebody who is incapable of doing it for themselves.

- David Letterman

I've always found that the poorer the places that I go, the more smiles I see, and the more happiness I see.

- **Michael Franti**

I see nothing wrong with the human trait to desire. In fact, I consider it integral to our success mechanism. Becoming attached to what we desire is what causes the trouble. If you must have it in order to be happy, then you are denying the happiness of the here and now.

- **Peter McWilliams**

It's up to you to be responsible for how you feel if you're not happy. Your happiness lies in your hands. You can't rely on a man to make you happy or complete you. That starts with you.

- **Taraji P. Henson**

There are other ways of finding satisfaction, recipes for human happiness, enjoyment, dignified and meaningful, gratifying life, than increased consumption that increases production.

- **Zygmunt Bauman**

Why does watching a dog be a dog fill one with happiness?

- **Jonathan Safran Foer**

It is the paradox of life that the way to miss pleasure is to seek it first. The very first condition of lasting happiness is that a life should be full of purpose, aiming at something outside self.

- Hugo Black

Genuine happiness comes from within, and often it comes in spontaneous feelings of joy.

- Andrew Weil

I think happiness comes from self-acceptance. We all try different things, and we find some comfortable sense of who we are. We look at our parents and learn and grow and move on. We change.

- Jamie Lee Curtis

I'd learned how much happiness money can bring you. Very little.

- Rick Pitino

We need to move into a culture of peace. What I hope to promote is the idea that we all need each other and that the greatest happiness in life is not how much we have but how much we give. That's a wealth that's priceless. You can't buy compassion.

- Herbie Hancock

In the scope of a happy life, a messy desk or an overstuffed coat closet is a trivial thing, yet I find - and I hear from other people that they agree - that getting rid of clutter gives a disproportionate boost to happiness.

- Gretchen Rubin

Only one thing has to change for us to know happiness in our lives: where we focus our attention.

- Greg Anderson

There are no plans that always work in life. For me, the secret to happiness is being positive and looking at the brighter side of my life.

- Karisma Kapoor

Life is made up of small pleasures. Happiness is made up of those tiny successes. The big ones come too infrequently. And if you don't collect all these tiny successes, the big ones don't really mean anything.

- Norman Lear

Happiness is a critical factor for work, and work is a critical factor for happiness. In one of those life-isn't-fair results, it turns out that the happy outperform the less happy. Happy people work more hours each week - and they work more in their free time, too.

- Gretchen Rubin

The more I travel around the world, the more I see people want the same thing - to be happy. We wouldn't be in a monetary system if we didn't have to work, so if my music can contribute to happiness, then that's my main responsibility.

- Jason Mraz

To have the sense of creative activity is the great happiness and the great proof of being alive.

- Matthew Arnold

I do not equate productivity to happiness. For most people, happiness in life is a massive amount of achievement plus a massive amount of appreciation. And you need both of those things.

- Timothy Ferriss

Happiness, or misery, is in the mind. It is the mind that lives.

- William Cobbett

As long as you are being true to yourself, you will always find happiness.

- Amber Riley

People are not on a truth quest; they are on a happiness quest. They will continue to attend your church - even if they don't share your beliefs - as long as they find the content engaging and helpful.

- Andy Stanley

It is the true duty of every man to promote the happiness of his fellow creatures to the utmost of his power.

- William Wilberforce

My parents - they've been my biggest influences and supporters since day one. They teach me every day that happiness comes from within and not from something outside of your heart.

- Shawn Johnson

Happiness exists only if you have a lot of people to share it with.

- Ranbir Kapoor

I think for me, happiness is crucial, but I think we think that happiness comes from amassing goods and getting things and being loved and being successful, when in fact my experience of happiness comes when you give everything away, when you serve people, when you're watching something you do make somebody happy - that's when happiness happens.

- Eve Ensler

There is one thing in this good old world that is positively sure - happiness is for all who strive to be happy - and those who laugh are happy. Everybody is eligible - you - me - the other fellow. Happiness is fundamentally a state of mind - not a state of body.

- Douglas Fairbanks

Happiness is not a matter of events; it depends upon the tides of the mind.

- Alice Meynell

I think if we want to find happiness by finding a life partner, then it's a little selfish. You should be complete within yourself, so that when you're in a relationship, you can give out happiness rather than expect it.

- Shahid Kapoor

My aim in life isn't so much the pursuit of happiness as the happiness of pursuit.

- Charles Saatchi

I'm an inherently happy person. It comes from the inside, which means you can achieve happiness under any circumstance.

- Patrick Duffy

I knew everything and received everything. But real happiness, is giving.

- Alain Delon

No true and permanent fame can be founded except in labors which promote the happiness of mankind.

- Charles Sumner

When you analyze happiness, it turns out that the way you spend your time is extremely important.

- Daniel Kahneman

Money cannot buy happiness.

- Frida Lyngstad

Happiness isn't a fortune in a cookie. It's deeper, wider, funnier, and more transporting than that.

- **Elvis Costello**

Action may not bring happiness but there is no happiness without action.

- **William James**

You look at your bank account, and you see the currency of love and happiness is more important than the currency of money.

- **Richie Sambora**

Doing nothing is happiness for children and misery for old men.

- **Victor Hugo**

Where fear is, happiness is not.

- **Lucius Annaeus Seneca**

I try to stress to my children that buying something never leads to true happiness.

- **Harlan Coben**

I really love being alive. I love my family and my work. I love the opportunity I have to do things. That's what happiness is.

- Michael J. Fox

I think happiness is a goal all of us can agree on. Let's face it - we all would like to be happy.

- Joyce Meyer

Remember that happiness is as contagious as gloom. It should be the first duty of those who are happy to let others know of their gladness.

- Maurice Maeterlinck

<u>Wealth</u>

Money can't buy happiness, but it can make you awfully comfortable while you're being miserable.
- Clare Boothe Luce

A little thought and a little kindness are often worth more than a great deal of money.
- John Ruskin

Money cannot buy peace of mind. It cannot heal ruptured relationships, or build meaning into a life that has none.
- Richard M. DeVos

A wise man should have money in his head, but not in his heart.
- Jonathan Swift

There are people who have money and people who are rich.
- Coco Chanel

A penny saved is a penny earned.

- Benjamin Franklin

After a certain point, money is meaningless. It ceases to be the goal. The game is what counts.

- Aristotle Onassis

A man in debt is so far a slave.

- Ralph Waldo Emerson

Do what you love and the money will follow.

- Marsha Sinetar

Money is only a tool. It will take you wherever you wish, but it will not replace you as the driver.

- Ayn Rand

Wealth is the ability to fully experience life.

- Henry David Thoreau

Money won't create success, the freedom to make it will.

- Nelson Mandela

The lack of money is the root of all evil.

- Mark Twain

Greed is not a financial issue. It's a heart issue.

- Andy Stanley

Real riches are the riches possessed inside.

- B. C. Forbes

Money is better than poverty, if only for financial reasons.

- Woody Allen

A bank is a place that will lend you money if you can prove that you don't need it.

- Bob Hope

A woman's best protection is a little money of her own.

- Clare Boothe Luce

Men make counterfeit money; in many more cases, money makes counterfeit men.

- Sydney J. Harris

All money means to me is a pride in accomplishment.

— **Ray Kroc**

It's a kind of spiritual snobbery that makes people think they can be happy without money.

— **Albert Camus**

My goal wasn't to make a ton of money. It was to build good computers.

— **Steve Wozniak**

A good reputation is more valuable than money.

— **Publilius Syrus**

Sometimes your best investments are the ones you don't make.

— **Donald Trump**

There's no such thing as a free lunch.

— **Milton Friedman**

I'd like to live as a poor man with lots of money.

— **Pablo Picasso**

I have no money, no resources, no hopes. I am the happiest man alive.

- **Henry Miller**

If you want to reap financial blessings, you have to sow financially.

- **Joel Osteen**

All riches have their origin in mind. Wealth is in ideas - not money.

- **Robert Collier**

Money equals freedom.

- **Kevin O'Leary**

It is more rewarding to watch money change the world than watch it accumulate.

- **Gloria Steinem**

Money often costs too much.

- **Ralph Waldo Emerson**

Money is the barometer of a society's virtue.

- **Ayn Rand**

A man with money is no match against a man on a mission.

- Doyle Brunson

It is not the creation of wealth that is wrong, but the love of money for its own sake.

- Margaret Thatcher

Money is always there but the pockets change; it is not in the same pockets after a change, and that is all there is to say about money.

- Gertrude Stein

If saving money is wrong, I don't want to be right!

- William Shatner

Money does not make you happy but it quiets the nerves.

- Sean O'Casey

Many people take no care of their money till they come nearly to the end of it, and others do just the same with their time.

- Johann Wolfgang von Goethe

Anybody who thinks money will make you happy, hasn't got money.

- David Geffen

Money is a strange business. People who haven't got it aim it strongly. People who have are full of troubles.

- Ayrton Senna

My pride fell with my fortunes.

- William Shakespeare

A man is usually more careful of his money than of his principles.

- Oliver Wendell Holmes, Jr.

If God has allowed me to earn so much money, it is because He knows I give it all away.

- Edith Piaf

We've got to put a lot of money into changing behavior.

- Bill Gates

All I ask is the chance to prove that money can't make me happy.

- Spike Milligan

We go to school to learn to work hard for money. I write books and create products that teach people how to have money work hard for them.

- Robert Kiyosaki

If you can count your money, you don't have a billion dollars.

- J. Paul Getty

You have to go broke three times to learn how to make a living.

- Casey Stengel

Affluence creates poverty.

- Marshall McLuhan

If the money we donate helps one child or can ease the pain of one parent, those funds are well spent.

- Carl Karcher

In suggesting gifts: Money is appropriate, and one size fits all.

- William Randolph Hearst

The safe way to double your money is to fold it over once and put it in your pocket.

- Kin Hubbard

Money's a horrid thing to follow, but a charming thing to meet.

- Henry James

Everyone needs a certain amount of money. Beyond that, we pursue money because we know how to obtain it. We don't necessarily know how to obtain happiness.

- Gregg Easterbrook

What counts is what you do with your money, not where it came from.

- Merton Miller

Put not your trust in money, but put your money in trust.

- Oliver Wendell Holmes, Sr.

Nothing is more dangerous to men than a sudden change of fortune.

- **Quintilian**

A man who gives his children habits of industry provides for them better than by giving them fortune.

- **Richard Whately**

Wealth flows from energy and ideas.

- **William Feather**

All my life I knew that there was all the money you could want out there. All you have to do is go after it.

- **Curtis Carlson**

It doesn't matter about money; having it, not having it. Or having clothes, or not having them. You're still left alone with yourself in the end.

- **Billy Idol**

A simple fact that is hard to learn is that the time to save money is when you have some.

- **Joe Moore**

If money was my only motivation, I would organize myself differently.

- Placido Domingo

Many good qualities are not sufficient to balance a single want - the want of money.

- Johann Georg Zimmermann

No man's credit is as good as his money.

- John Dewey

Money just draws flies.

- Mahalia Jackson

Money is our madness, our vast collective madness.

- D. H. Lawrence

The foundation of a financial fresh start actually has nothing to do with money or specific financial dos and don'ts.

- Suze Orman

Many folks think they aren't good at earning money, when what they don't know is how to use it.

- Frank A. Clark

I've made all my money on my own without my family and I work very hard.

- Paris Hilton

Money: power at its most liquid.

- Mason Cooley

For I can raise no money by vile means.

- William Shakespeare

I think everything depends on money.

- Alan Bean

Who covets more is evermore a slave.

- Robert Herrick

I'd rather lose my own money than someone else's.

- Dean Kamen

Money is a mechanism for control.

- David Korten

Very few people can afford to be poor.

- George Bernard Shaw

A fool and his money are soon parted.

- Thomas Tusser

I am fiercely loyal to those willing to put their money where my mouth is.

- Paul Harvey

Marrying into money was not a good thing for me.

- Anna Nicole Smith

Sooner or later, we sell out for money.

- Tony Randall

The creditor hath a better memory than the debtor.

- James Howell

Those who are of the opinion that money will do everything may reasonably be expected to do everything for money.

- E. F. L. Wood, 1st Earl of Halifax

Business is other people's money.

- Delphine de Girardin

The greatest luxury of riches is that they enable you to escape so much good advice.

- Arthur Helps

Wealth and want equally harden the human heart.

- Theodore Parker

If I have enough money to eat I'm good.

- Shia LaBeouf

A fool and his money are lucky enough to get together in the first place.

- Stanley Weiser

An important lever for sustained action in tackling poverty and reducing hunger is money.

- Gro Harlem Brundtland

I don't think business news is just for old white men with money.

- Neil Cavuto

The most efficient labor-saving device is still money.

- Franklin P. Jones

My favorite things in life don't cost any money. It's really clear that the most precious resource we all have is time.

- Steve Jobs

To give real service you must add something which cannot be bought or measured with money, and that is sincerity and integrity.

- Douglas Adams

Money won't buy happiness, but it will pay the salaries of a large research staff to study the problem.

- Bill Vaughan

The greatest legacy one can pass on to one's children and grandchildren is not money or other material things accumulated in one's life, but rather a legacy of character and faith.

- Billy Graham

A successful man is one who makes more money than his wife can spend. A successful woman is one who can find such a man.

- Lana Turner

You want 21 percent risk free? Pay off your credit cards.

- Andrew Tobias

Friends and good manners will carry you where money won't go.

- Margaret Walker

A business that makes nothing but money is a poor business.

- Henry Ford

The American Dream is still alive out there, and hard work will get you there. You don't necessarily need to have an Ivy League education or to have millions of dollars startup money. It can be done with an idea, hard work and determination.

- Bill Rancic

Encouragement to others is something everyone can give. Somebody needs what you have to give. It may not be your money; it may be your time. It may be your listening ear. It may be your arms to encourage. It may be your smile to uplift. Who knows?

- Joel Osteen

The most valuable lesson I've ever learned in my life is that life is about family and friends, not about material things or any of that. It's about enjoying your life. If you have no family, no friends to enjoy it with, it don't matter how much you have, how much success you have, how much fame you have, how much money you have, it doesn't matter.

- Vanilla Ice

Let us more and more insist on raising funds of love, of kindness, of understanding, of peace. Money will come if we seek first the Kingdom of God - the rest will be given.

- Mother Teresa

What's money? A man is a success if he gets up in the morning and goes to bed at night and in between does what he wants to do.

- Bob Dylan

Money and success don't change people; they merely amplify what is already there.

- Will Smith

If money is your hope for independence you will never have it. The only real security that a man will have in this world is a reserve of knowledge, experience, and ability.

- Henry Ford

If you don't have integrity, you have nothing. You can't buy it. You can have all the money in the world, but if you are not a moral and ethical person, you really have nothing.

- Henry Kravis

It is not the employer who pays the wages. Employers only handle the money. It is the customer who pays the wages.

- Henry Ford

You are your greatest asset. Put your time, effort and money into training, grooming, and encouraging your greatest asset.

- **Tom Hopkins**

Let us not be satisfied with just giving money. Money is not enough, money can be got, but they need your hearts to love them. So, spread your love everywhere you go.

- **Mother Teresa**

My mom worked at McDonald's, and she decided she wanted to make more money, so she got into the management program at McDonald's. And that's how you move up the chain. It's not by demanding that minimum wage is raised; it's by actually acquiring the skills. That's the way that people get ahead in life.

- **Raul Labrador**

Money can buy you a fine dog, but only love can make him wag his tail.

- **Kinky Friedman**

The circulation of confidence is better than the circulation of money.

- **James Madison**

If you work just for money, you'll never make it, but if you love what you're doing and you always put the customer first, success will be yours.

- Ray Kroc

Money can't buy life.

- Bob Marley

Money doesn't mean anything to me. I've made a lot of money, but I want to enjoy life and not stress myself building my bank account. I give lots away and live simply, mostly out of a suitcase in hotels. We all know that good health is much more important.

- Keanu Reeves

Teamwork is so important that it is virtually impossible for you to reach the heights of your capabilities or make the money that you want without becoming very good at it.

- Brian Tracy

Success is having to worry about every damn thing in the world, except money.

- Johnny Cash

I think the person who takes a job in order to live - that is to say, for the money - has turned himself into a slave.
- Joseph Campbell

Money is not the only answer, but it makes a difference.
- Barack Obama

All money is a matter of belief.
- Adam Smith

Too many people spend money they haven't earned to buy things they don't want to impress people they don't like.
- Will Rogers

Money was never a big motivation for me, except as a way to keep score. The real excitement is playing the game.
- Donald Trump

Work like you don't need the money. Love like you've never been hurt. Dance like nobody's watching.
- Satchel Paige

I have ways of making money that you know nothing of.
- John D. Rockefeller

If you love friends, you will serve your friends. If you love community, you will serve your community. If you love money, you will serve your money. And if you love only yourself, you will serve only yourself. And you will have only yourself.

- Stephen Colbert

To be poor does not mean you lack the means to extend charity to another. You may lack money or food, but you have the gift of friendship to overwhelm the loneliness that grips the lives of so many.

- Stanley Hauerwas

I know of nothing more despicable and pathetic than a man who devotes all the hours of the waking day to the making of money for money's sake.

- John D. Rockefeller

If money helps a man to do good to others, it is of some value; but if not, it is simply a mass of evil, and the sooner it is got rid of, the better.

- Swami Vivekananda

The Berlin Wall wasn't the only barrier to fall after the collapse of the Soviet Union and the end of the Cold War. Traditional barriers to the flow of money, trade, people and ideas also fell.

- Fareed Zakaria

Recommend virtue to your children; it alone, not money, can make them happy. I speak from experience.

- Ludwig van Beethoven

The reason we have poverty is that we have no imagination. There are a great many people accumulating what they think is vast wealth, but it's only money... they don't know how to enjoy it, because they have no imagination.

- Alan Watts

I would say the most satisfying thing actually is watching my three children each pick up on their own interests and work many more hours per week than most people that have jobs at trying to intelligently give away that money in fields that they particularly care about.

- Warren Buffett

Time is money.

- Benjamin Franklin

If we pollute the air, water and soil that keep us alive and well, and destroy the biodiversity that allows natural systems to function, no amount of money will save us.

- David Suzuki

There is a gigantic difference between earning a great deal of money and being rich.

- Marlene Dietrich

For a successful entrepreneur it can mean extreme wealth. But with extreme wealth comes extreme responsibility. And the responsibility for me is to invest in creating new businesses, create jobs, employ people, and to put money aside to tackle issues where we can make a difference.

- Richard Branson

To get rich, you have to be making money while you're asleep.

- David Bailey

Most people work just hard enough not to get fired and get paid just enough money not to quit.

- George Carlin

Here in the big city people spend their time thinking about work and about money; they don't give some value to friendships and it can be depressing.

- Adriana Lima

Money doesn't make you happy. I now have $50 million but I was just as happy when I had $48 million.

- Arnold Schwarzenegger

The writer must earn money in order to be able to live and to write, but he must by no means live and write for the purpose of making money.

- Karl Marx

I don't care about having money. It's about being happy, man.

- Skrillex

Athletes and musicians make astronomical amounts of money. People get paid $100 million to throw a baseball! Shouldn't we all take less and pass some of that money onto others? Think about fire-fighters, teachers and policemen. We should celebrate people that are intellectually smart and trying to make this world a better place.

- Kid Rock

My father was an immigrant who literally walked across Europe to get out of Russia. He fought in World War I. He was wounded in action. My father was a great success even though he never had money. He was a very determined man, a great role model.

- Arlen Specter

The first time you marry for love, the second for money, and the third for companionship.

- Jackie Kennedy

The key to making money is to stay invested.

- Suze Orman

Money doesn't talk, it swears.

- Bob Dylan

That should be the measure of success for everyone. It's not money, it's not fame, it's not celebrity; my index of success is happiness.

- Lupe Fiasco

I'm not a driven businessman, but a driven artist. I never think about money. Beautiful things make money.

- Lord Acton

Money doesn't buy elegance. You can take an inexpensive sheath, add a pretty scarf, gray shoes, and a wonderful bag, and it will always be elegant.

- Carolina Herrera

Spirituality does two things for you. One, you are forced to become more selfless, two, you trust to providence. The opposite of a spiritual man is a materialist. If I was a materialist I would be making lots of money doing endorsements, doing cricket commentary. I have no interest in that.

- Imran Khan

Making money is a happiness. And that's a great incentive. Making other people happy is a super-happiness.

- Muhammad Yunus

Of the billionaires I have known, money just brings out the basic traits in them. If they were jerks before they had money, they are simply jerks with a billion dollars.

- Warren Buffett

Never spend your money before you have earned it.

- Thomas Jefferson

The way to make money is to buy when blood is running in the streets.

- John D. Rockefeller

A guy who has all the money he needs and never faced any hard times, he won't have any character. But when you've had it tough and you've had it rough and you thought you were at the end of the rope and you work your way out of it, that's the way you build character.

- Bobby Bowden

There are two things people want more than sex and money... recognition and praise.

- Mary Kay Ash

Knowledge is like money: to be of value it must circulate, and in circulating it can increase in quantity and, hopefully, in value.

- Louis L'Amour

All the money in the world can't buy you back good health.

- Reba McEntire

Good grooming is integral and impeccable style is a must. If you don't look the part, no one will want to give you time or money.

- **Daymond John**

My restaurants are never opened on Thanksgiving; I want my staff to spend time with their family if they can. My feeling is, if I can't figure out how to make money the rest of the year so that my workers can enjoy the holidays, then I don't deserve to be an owner.

- **Michael Symon**

I've had an exciting time; I married for love and got a little money along with it.

- **Rose Kennedy**

Money is a very important tool to make a big difference in people's life. It is positive or negative depending on the values.

- **Shiv Khera**

There's nothing more satisfying than seeing a happy and smiling child. I always help in any way I can, even if it's just by signing an autograph. A child's smile is worth more than all the money in the world.

- **Lionel Messi**

A real gentleman, even if he loses everything he owns, must show no emotion. Money must be so far beneath a gentleman that it is hardly worth troubling about.

- Fyodor Dostoevsky

I would prefer to have no money but to have a nice family and good friends around.

- Li Na

Advertising: the science of arresting the human intelligence long enough to get money from it.

- Stephen Leacock

I do not think I am successful just because I have money. I'm successful because I love who I am and I have no regrets, and I'm successful because I have a great heart and I have compassion and I care and I would be happy with or without money.

- Suze Orman

There is a soak-the-rich attitude in the air, a feeling that if you have a lot of money you must have got it by some ghastly means. I can quite happily say there was never any family money. All the money we got was mine, just from writing books.

- Terry Pratchett

When you ain't got no money, you gotta get an attitude.

- Richard Pryor

If a man has wealth, he has to make a choice, because there is the money heaping up. He can keep it together in a bunch, and then leave it for others to administer after he is dead. Or he can get it into action and have fun, while he is still alive. I prefer getting it into action and adapting it to human needs, and making the plan work.

- George Eastman

Time is more value than money. You can get more money, but you cannot get more time.

- Jim Rohn

Time well spent results in more money to spend, more money to save, and more time to vacation.

- Zig Ziglar

Today, the concept of business is to make money. Making money is the name of the business.

- Muhammad Yunus

I think it's way harder when you have success, 'cause people tend to not treat you the same or look at you the same because they see the success or the money you make.

- **Meek Mill**

I've never chased money. It's always been about what I can do to motivate and inspire people.

- **Tyler Perry**

One does not need buildings, money, power, or status to practice the Art of Peace. Heaven is right where you are standing, and that is the place to train.

- **Morihei Ueshiba**

I'm not looking for career attention, for more success, more money. I'm just singing songs I chose because I love them.

- **Celine Dion**

Disneyland is a work of love. We didn't go into Disneyland just with the idea of making money.

- **Walt Disney**

Waste your money and you're only out of money, but waste your time and you've lost a part of your life.

- **Michael LeBoeuf**

The worship of the golden calf of old has found a new and heartless image in the cult of money and the dictatorship of an economy which is faceless and lacking any truly human goal.

- Pope Francis

It's not about how skinny you are or how much money or how many diamonds you have - that's the fluff that people sometimes look at as being the main thing. It's about understanding that the things that make you fabulous are all inside of you.

- Kimora Lee Simmons

There is no class so pitiably wretched as that which possesses money and nothing else.

- Andrew Carnegie

If you stop at general math, you're only going to make general math money.

- Snoop Dogg

Your goal should be to pay off your credit card bills in full at the end of each month and set aside money toward your emergency savings.

- Suze Orman

A lot of people feel trapped by circumstance, by the expectations of others or the perception that they need a lot of money. They would like to have a different direction in their lives, but they're held back by fear or desires that are incompatible with that freedom.

- Roz Savage

I really don't like talking about money. All I can say is that the Good Lord must have wanted me to have it.

- Larry Bird

Don't cry about money, it never cries for you.

- Kevin O'Leary

People ask how can a Jewish kid from the Bronx do preppy clothes? Does it have to do with class and money? It has to do with dreams.

- Ralph Lauren

You use your money to buy privacy because during most of your life you aren't allowed to be normal.

- Johnny Depp

You want to buy cars and houses and castles, all of that's on you and how America has systematized your mind to be into materialism. Hip-hop ain't got nothing to do with that. I'm glad that anybody making money has picked themselves up - I just want them to give some of it back to the community.

- Afrika Bambaataa

We can all be successful and make money, but when we die, that ends. But when you are significant is when you help other people be successful. That lasts many a lifetime.

- Lou Holtz

I don't believe the most successful people are the ones who got the best grades, got into the best schools, or made the most money.

- Ben Stein

You reach a point where you don't work for money.

- Walt Disney

If you put all your strength and faith and vigor into a job and try to do the best you can, the money will come.

- Lawrence Welk

A runner must run with dreams in his heart, not money in his pocket.

- Emil Zatopek

Enthusiasm is the greatest asset you can possess, for it can take you further than money, power or influence.

- Dada Vaswani

The day, water, sun, moon, night - I do not have to purchase these things with money.

- Plautus

You have reached the pinnacle of success as soon as you become uninterested in money, compliments, or publicity.

- Thomas Wolfe

Always remember, money isn't everything - but also remember to make a lot of it before talking such fool nonsense.

- Earl Wilson

Philanthropy is not about giving money but about solving problems. While well-meaning, the idea of writing a check and calling it 'philanthropy' is extremely short-sighted and unfortunately, extremely pervasive.

- Naveen Jain

I definitely wanted to earn my freedom. But the primary motivation wasn't making money, but making an impact.

- Sean Parker

If we were motivated by money, we would have sold the company a long time ago and ended up on a beach.

- Larry Page

I don't make deals for the money. I've got enough, much more than I'll ever need. I do it to do it.

- Donald Trump

Do not hire a man who does your work for money, but him who does it for love of it.

- Henry David Thoreau

Money is in some respects life's fire: it is a very excellent servant, but a terrible master.

- P. T. Barnum

I'm fulfilled in what I do. I never thought that a lot of money or fine clothes - the finer things of life - would make you happy. My concept of happiness is to be filled in a spiritual sense.

— **Coretta Scott King**

I own about 300 pairs of shoes. When I start to go over 300, I have mini-sales from my closet and give the money to charity. It's my way of recycling; I feel like I can give back to the universe.

— **Stacy London**

Music has always been my back door to life. It is important for people to find something that excites them. I like the concept that if you do what excites you, you will be rewarded generously, whatever form reward takes, which is not necessarily money.

— **Brandon Boyd**

Maybe a person's time would be as well spent raising food as raising money to buy food.

— **Frank A. Clark**

With the amount of money I have, it's difficult raising children the way I was raised.

— **Adam Sandler**

If it was all about me, I'd do a whole lot of pop records, make a whole lot of money, just rake in the dough. But it's never been all about me. It's all about being a voice for the voiceless. People who can't speak for themselves, who don't have a mic, don't have a say.

- Ice Cube

There's something very visceral about watching people beg for money. It's powerful.

- Kevin O'Leary

Nobody ever lost money taking a profit.

- Bernard Baruch

Successful people make money. It's not that people who make money become successful, but that successful people attract money. They bring success to what they do.

- Wayne Dyer

My challenge when I came back was to face the young talent, dissect their games, and show them maybe that they needed to learn more about the game than just the money aspect.

- Michael Jordan

Money won't make you happy... but everybody wants to find out for themselves.

- **Zig Ziglar**

When you first get money, you buy all these things so no one thinks you're mean, and you spread it around. You get a chauffeur and you find yourself thrown around the back of this car and you think, I was happier when I had my own little car! I could drive myself!

- **Paul McCartney**

Time is money says the proverb, but turn it around and you get a precious truth. Money is time.

- **George Gissing**

I started doing a paper round when I was about 10. I started earning 10 pounds a week and then I was obsessed with earning money until I was about 15.

- **Robert Pattinson**

If you can actually count your money, then you're not a rich man.

- **J. Paul Getty**

Try paying the bills with love. The idea I am trying to espouse is that you can have both love and money, and be rich and generous.

- T. Harv Eker

The only rich person is a person who is rich in spirit. I have no money deposit. I have only beauty deposit.

- Imelda Marcos

The function of the press in society is to inform, but its role in society is to make money.

- A. J. Liebling

I was the second of six kids. I wouldn't say we were poor; we had no money. That's different.

- Martha Stewart

Money is the medium of exchange, and it's how you make things happen. To say you hate it is some farfetched, idealistic crap.

- Bobby Seale

Look at our society. Everyone wants to be thin, but nobody wants to diet. Everyone wants to live long, but few will exercise. Everybody wants money, yet seldom will anyone budget or control their spending.

- John C. Maxwell

Making money is a hobby that will complement any other hobbies you have, beautifully.

- Scott Alexander

First and foremost I am a drummer. After that, I'm other things... But I didn't play drums to make money.

- Ringo Starr

What saddens me is the corruption of youth and beauty, and the loss of soul, which is only replaced by money.

- Lisa Bonet

Companies should not have a singular view of profitability. There needs to be a balance between commerce and social responsibility... The companies that are authentic about it will wind up as the companies that make more money.

- Howard Schultz

An athlete cannot run with money in his pockets. He must run with hope in his heart and dreams in his head.

- Emil Zatopek

You aren't wealthy until you have something money can't buy.

- Garth Brooks

Looking back, yes, I made too many comebacks. But each comeback I was 100 percent sure that I would win. I never came back for the money, because I didn't need it. The adulation I was getting anyway in other spheres. But I'm a guy who likes to see how close he can get to the edge of the mountain - that's what makes me tick.

- Sugar Ray Leonard

The big difference between sex for money and sex for free is that sex for money usually costs a lot less.

- Brendan Behan

I think a lot of times it's not money that's the primary motivation factor; it's the passion for your job and the professional and personal satisfaction that you get out of doing what you do that motivates you.

- Martin Yan

Like anything else that happens on its own, the act of writing is beyond currency. Money is great stuff to have, but when it comes to the act of creation, the best thing is not to think of money too much. It constipates the whole process.

- Stephen King

Money is neither my god nor my devil. It is a form of energy that tends to make us more of who we already are, whether it's greedy or loving.

- Dan Millman

Time and money spent in helping men to do more for themselves is far better than mere giving.

- Henry Ford

Money is human happiness in the abstract; he, then, who is no longer capable of enjoying human happiness in the concrete devotes himself utterly to money.

- Arthur Schopenhauer

The companies that survive longest are the one's that work out what they uniquely can give to the world not just growth or money but their excellence, their respect for others, or their ability to make people happy. Some call those things a soul.

- Charles Handy

Making money is easy. It is. The difficult thing in life is not making it, it's keeping it.

- John McAfee

Money has no utility to me beyond a certain point.

- Bill Gates

I always try to be smart. I try to treat all the money I'm making like it's the last time I'm going to make it.

- Eminem

I don't want to make money; I just want to be wonderful.

- Marilyn Monroe

My philosophy is that if I have any money I invest it in new ventures and not have it sitting around.

- Richard Branson

To fulfil a dream, to be allowed to sweat over lonely labor, to be given a chance to create, is the meat and potatoes of life. The money is the gravy.

- Bette Davis

Friendship and money: oil and water.

- Mario Puzo

I was a common man, and I will always remain a common man. No amount of stardom will ever consume my soul. Money comes, money goes. Fame comes, fame goes. I believe every human being is a celebrity in their own right.

- A. R. Rahman

When we die our money, fame, and honors will be meaningless. We own nothing in this world. Everything we think we own is in reality only being loaned to us until we die. And on our deathbed at the moment of death, no one but God can save our souls.

- Michael Huffington

I always thought money was something just to make me happy. But I've learned that I feel better being able to help my folks, 'cause we never had nothing. So just to see them excited about my career is more of a blessing than me actually having it for myself.

- Kendrick Lamar

Sure, I have friends, plenty of friends, and they all come around wantin' to borrow money. I've always been generous with my friends and family, with money, but selfish with the important stuff like love.

- Richard Pryor

Work isn't to make money; you work to justify life.

- Marc Chagall

I have a fantastic relationship with money. I use it to buy my freedom.

- Gianni Versace

America believes in education: the average professor earns more money in a year than a professional athlete earns in a whole week.

- Evan Esar

The secret of my success is that I make other people money. And, never ever, ever, ever be ashamed about trying to earn as much as possible for yourself, if the person you're working with is also making money. That's life!

- Simon Cowell

Money has no grey areas. You either make it or you lose it.
- Kevin O'Leary

Unless you're living on the street and surviving on a diet of discarded turkey drumsticks, there's no point in being gloomy. We've spent too long trying to cheer ourselves up by spending money on brightly coloured things we don't really need. We've stopped using our imaginations.
- Jarvis Cocker

No hours, nor amount of labor, nor amount of money would deter me from giving the best that there was in me.
- Colonel Sanders

Don't stay in bed, unless you can make money in bed.
- George Burns

Expensive clothes are a waste of money.
- Meryl Streep

I believe God, Jesus, died that we not just go to Heaven but that we excel in this life. I never think you make money your goal... God wants you to excel. Just keep Him in first place, and God will open up doors you never dreamed of.

- Joel Osteen

Money motivates neither the best people, nor the best in people. It can move the body and influence the mind, but it cannot touch the heart or move the spirit; that is reserved for belief, principle, and morality.

- Dee Hock

Despite their good intentions, today's businesses are missing an opportunity to integrate social responsibility and day-to-day business objectives - to do good and make money simultaneously.

- Cindy Gallop

Money is like an arm or leg - use it or lose it.

- Henry Ford

The shortest period of time lies between the minute you put some money away for a rainy day and the unexpected arrival of rain.

- Jane Bryant Quinn

If you are worried about job security and do not have an adequate emergency fund (ideally eight months' worth of living expenses stashed away in a federally insured bank or credit union), you need to focus more on saving money than paying down the balance on your credit cards.

- Suze Orman

So much business is based on the belief that we should do whatever we can within legal limits to make as much money as we can. Ben & Jerry's was based on values, and we try to operate a business that not just sells ice cream but partners with all our stakeholders - whether that's suppliers or customers - to bring about a more sustainable world.

- Jerry Greenfield

Money is not required to buy one necessity of the soul.

- Henry David Thoreau

Speculation is only a word covering the making of money out of the manipulation of prices, instead of supplying goods and services.

- Henry Ford

Nothing that is God's is obtainable by money.

- Tertullian

Our idea is to serve everybody, including people with little money.

- Ingvar Kamprad

Apple's goal isn't to make money. Our goal is to design and develop and bring to market good products.

- Jonathan Ive

Money isn't the most important thing in life, but it's reasonably close to oxygen on the 'gotta have it' scale.

- Zig Ziglar

Good nature is worth more than knowledge, more than money, more than honor, to the persons who possess it.

- Henry Ward Beecher

We need to shift from an economic organizing principle for human civilization, to a humanitarian organizing principle. Making money more important than your own children is a pathological way for an individual to run their affairs, and it's a pathological way for a society to run its affairs.

- Marianne Williamson

Success must never be measured by how much money you have.

- **Zig Ziglar**

Money is usually attracted, not pursued.

- **Jim Rohn**

Remember that credit is money.

- **Benjamin Franklin**

Money is like manure. You have to spread it around or it smells.

- **J. Paul Getty**

People spend time worrying about things they think they have to have and lose perception of what they do have. You can have all the money and material things you want. If you aren't here to enjoy them, what good do they do?

- **Eric Davis**

The music business is motivated by money. Music is motivated by energy and feelings.

- **Erykah Badu**

To this day, I am the least materialistic person I know, because my father didn't raise me to just go out and buy this or that car. The only reason I wanted to make money as an actor was because I'm passionate about food!

- Hugh Jackman

The only thing money gives you is the freedom of not worrying about money.

- Johnny Carson

I don't want to make money; I want to make a difference.

- Lady Gaga

Before borrowing money from a friend it's best to decide which you need most.

- Joe Moore

No, not rich. I am a poor man with money, which is not the same thing.

- Gabriel Garcia Marquez

My children were taught at an early age how money works and that it comes from hard work. They've been on a commission - not an allowance - since they were little. They learned that if they worked around the house, they got paid. If they didn't work, they didn't get paid.

- Dave Ramsey

Money does not guarantee success.

- Jose Mourinho

Starting out to make money is the greatest mistake in life. Do what you feel you have a flair for doing, and if you are good enough at it, the money will come.

- Greer Garson

There are some things that you can fulfil with money, but at the end of the day these are not the things that make you happy. It is the small things that make life good.

- Sebastian Vettel

If you wake up deciding what you want to give versus what you're going to get, you become a more successful person. In other words, if you want to make money, you have to help someone else make money.

- Russell Simmons

People who get trapped in the tunnel vision of making money think that is all there is to life.

- Felix Dennis

Fame was thrilling only until it became gruelling. Money was fun only until you ran out of things to buy.

- Gloria Swanson

The goal isn't how much money you make, but how much you help people.

- Blake Mycoskie

God wants us to prosper financially, to have plenty of money, to fulfil the destiny He has laid out for us.

- Joel Osteen

It is a kind of spiritual snobbery that makes people think they can be happy without money.

- Albert Camus

Matters of the heart are important to me. All this materialism and all the money and wealth are things that you don't take to the grave. One day you have it. The next day you don't.

- Shari Arison

You don't want to have so much money going toward your mortgage every month that you can't enjoy life or take care of your other financial responsibilities.

- Dave Ramsey

I always was a rich person because money's not related to happiness.

- Paulo Coelho

If you don't want to work you have to work to earn enough money so that you won't have to work.

- Ogden Nash

The darkest hour in any man's life is when he sits down to plan how to get money without earning it.

- Horace Greeley

Time is more valuable than money, because time is irreplaceable.

- John C. Maxwell

A rich man is nothing but a poor man with money.

- W. C. Fields

When I chased after money, I never had enough. When I got my life on purpose and focused on giving of myself and everything that arrived into my life, then I was prosperous.

- Wayne Dyer

Prospering just doesn't have to do with money.

- Joel Osteen

The highest use of capital is not to make more money, but to make money do more for the betterment of life.

- Henry Ford

I believe enlightenment or revelation comes in daily life. I look for joy, the peace of action. You need action. I'd have stopped writing years ago if it were for the money.

- Paulo Coelho

No woman marries for money; they are all clever enough, before marrying a millionaire, to fall in love with him first.

- Cesare Pavese

False riches, consisting of money, houses and lands, acquired by selfish means at cost to others and thereafter used selfishly, are almost always used for the oppression of other persons.

- Joseph Franklin Rutherford

We do not have a money problem in America. We have a values and priorities problem.

- Marian Wright Edelman

Find something in life that you love doing. If you make a lot of money, that's a bonus, and if you don't, you still won't hate going to work.

- Jeff Foxworthy

You've got to tell your money what to do or it will leave.

- Dave Ramsey

The foundation of a financial fresh start actually has nothing to do with money or specific financial dos and don'ts. The first, and most difficult, step is to absolve yourself and your spouse or partner of any guilt.

- Suze Orman

Much ingenuity with a little money is vastly more profitable and amusing than much money without ingenuity.

- Arnold Bennett

Often people attempt to live their lives backwards; they try to have more things, or more money, in order to do more of what they want, so they will be happier.

- Margaret Young

The great trouble with baseball today is that most of the players are in the game for the money and that's it, not for the love of it, the excitement of it, the thrill of it.

- Ty Cobb

Life is a game. Money is how we keep score.

- Ted Turner

Human beings are much bigger than just making money.

- Muhammad Yunus

If you're planning only to make money and nothing else, you'll be broke.

- Haile Gebrselassie

There are a lot of people with a lot of money, and I'm amazed they don't understand what a great pleasure it can be to give.

- Robert Mondavi

It's good to have money and the things that money can buy, but it's good, too, to check up once in a while and make sure that you haven't lost the things that money can't buy.

- George Horace Lorimer

The tragedy is that there is so much more incentive - money - to destroy the ecology than there is to preserve it.

- Paul Watson

Cursed be he above all others who's enslaved by love of money. Money takes the place of brothers, Money takes the place of parents, Money brings us war and slaughter.

- Anacreon

When I decided to be a musician I reckoned that that was going to be the way of less profit, less money. I was sort of giving up the idea of making a lot of money. It was what I loved to do. I would have done it anyway. If I'd had to work at Taco Bell I'd have still been out at night trying to play music.

- Tom Petty

The modern banking system manufactures money out of nothing.

- Josiah Stamp

Money isn't everything. Do you get married because of money? Do you have kids because of money?

- Walter Payton

To have done anything just for money is to have been truly idle.

- Henry David Thoreau

Don't bring your need to the marketplace, bring your skill. If you don't feel well, tell your doctor, but not the marketplace. If you need money, go to the bank, but not the marketplace.

- Jim Rohn

Why is there so much month left at the end of the money?

- John Barrymore

Money without brains is always dangerous.

- Napoleon Hill

Measure your wealth by what you'd have left if you lost all your money.

- H. Jackson Brown, Jr.

If a person gets his attitude toward money straight, it will help straighten out almost every other area in his life.

- Billy Graham

You can't get rid of poverty by giving people money.

- P. J. O'Rourke

I have a problem with too much money. I can't reinvest it fast enough, and because I reinvest it, more money comes in. Yes, the rich do get richer.

- Robert Kiyosaki

Our greatest lack is not money for any undertaking, but rather ideas, If the ideas are good, cash will somehow flow to where it is needed.

- Robert H. Schuller

Economy does not lie in sparing money, but in spending it wisely.

- Thomas Huxley

It is easy to be independent when you've got money. But to be independent when you haven't got a thing, that's the Lord's test.

- Mahalia Jackson

Getting money is not all a man's business: to cultivate kindness is a valuable part of the business of life.

- Samuel Johnson

I don't think the money people in Hollywood have ever thought I was normal, but I am dedicated to my work and that's what counts.

- Angelina Jolie

Why are people unemployed? Because there is no work. Why is there no work? Because people are not buying products and services. Why are people not buying products and services? Because they have no money. Why do people have no money? Because they are unemployed.

- Craig Bruce

Money is a handmaiden, if thou knowest how to use it; a mistress, if thou knowest not.

- Horace

I am a very rich person. I'm just waiting for the money to arrive.

- Robert Jamgotchian

www.ingramcontent.com/pod-product-compliance
Lightning Source LLC
Chambersburg PA
CBHW071348280526
45787CB00001B/258